HOME BUYING WITHOUT BANKS

BYRON HOLMES

DISCLAIMER

The ideas described herein are suggestions for possible ways of buying a home, financing it, etc.. There is no guarantee that any of these ideas will produce the desired results or that some of these ideas are legal in your particular state, province, or country.

It is your responsibility to look into any legal ramifications that may result in your activity. It is recommended that you seek professional legal advise with regard to any contracts you may choose to make.

Author of:

Simple Ways To Make Money.

*To my wife, whose help and
inspiration are invaluable.*

CONTENTS

INTRODUCTION

I've been asked: "How can anyone buy a house without a bank loan?" Oh sure, you can buy a house with all cash. But what I'm talking about in this book is buying a house with financing that doesn't involve you going hat in hand to a bank hoping that if you jump through enough hoops, they'll actually give you a minute of their time.

I'm sure you already know, banks have greatly tightened their lending standards to the point where a borrower has to have an incredibly high credit score and proof of a long term salaried job in a secure business. Good luck if your self-employed.

Over the last few years, banks have done a 180 degree switch. There was a time not too long ago when it seemed like all that was required of you to get a bank loan was that you be able to sign your name. Now banks are obsessed with your credit score and proving you have a rock solid job with so much income you don't really need their money. This has left too many of us out in the cold.

Banks used to be in the business to make loans. Now their money appears to be flowing into high risk overseas investments and exotic financial instrument trades.

So what is there to do if you want to buy a house, to own your own home and the banks take one look at you and show you the door? Well, there are alternatives. And these are available to whoever you are and whatever you do. This book will allow you to see what can be done to fulfill your goal of owning a home.

The recession has been hard. For too many it has been a real crisis, with people losing jobs and even losing their homes. I wrote this book because I believe that with a little knowledge and some handy information you can overcome the many obstacles that now hamper buying and owning a home.

Is it wise to buy now?

We are in a downturn in the real estate market. Some think that buying now is fool-hardy. But, this is actually a good time to purchase your home. Properties are priced lower now than they have been for many years. Many sellers are very anxious to unload their properties. And they are ready and willing to deal. This makes for an ideal opportunity for the creative buyer.

"Yes, you say, but the real estate market is uncertain." But, my response is that in the long run properties in most places do appreciate. They do eventually go up. Despite the downturn in the market, real estate in parts of the country is more valuable than it was ten years ago.

Depending on location, real estate will go back up. It is a commodity that almost everyone seeks to own. The population in this country is always growing. More housing will always be needed. Will Rogers, a famous comedian / commentator from the past, said: "Invest in land, they ain't making any more of it." Good real estate is a limited commodity. Desirable areas of the country are always going to be a good investment. Increasing demand in areas of insufficient housing supply will eventually cause higher real estate prices.

There is a good quotation from the National Association of Realtors: "Under all is the land. Upon its wise utilization and widely allocated ownership depend the survival and growth of free institutions and of our civilization."

Real estate is an essential support of our economy. When it fails, the whole economy goes down. When it is prosperous, most other aspects of our economy do well.

Opportunity:

The Chinese character for "crisis" is a combination of two different characters. One symbolizes "danger," the other "opportunity." Recessions can be opportunities for us to move forward in our lives.

With the recession came change. And where there is change, there is opportunity. It is important to be aware of this so you will be open to the new possibilities that can lead to your new home.

In this book, I offer ideas for buying a home without having to deal with banks. Here you will find proven methods to achieve that dream of home ownership. You will see that life does not have to be lived from one rental to another – living at the whim of a landlord who may keep raising rents even in bad times.

I believe everyone deserves a life free of fear and uncertainty about where they'll be living tomorrow. You can use the techniques offered in this book as stepping stones to home ownership without dependance on the manipulations of powerful greedy banks.

It happened before:

I guess I was about eight, maybe nine, I remember my granddad telling me stories about the Great Depression. He recounted about the hard times when he would leave his unpaid bills in a special drawer until they were properly "seasoned," like a good wine that needs to be "aged."

One of his stories had to do with the house my grandparents had lived in. They, like millions of others were unable to pay the mortgage. They had to quietly sweat out each day wondering if they would be left homeless.

As he told the story, I could see genuine pain in his eyes. When he got to the part where the bank was about to take his house away, I asked. "What happen to your house, grandpa?" That is when his serious face would break into a smile of relief. "FDR bought up all the past due mortgages and refinanced our house so that those of us – and there were a lot – who were down on their luck, could afford the payments. Your grandma and I were able to keep our home."

Those were different times and even though I know that the President Roosevelt himself hadn't personally bought up all the troubled mortgages in the country, I did understand the impact his decisions had not only on my grandparent's lives, but the lives of my parents and even me.

Today experts in economics have tried to untangle the financial chaos that has so harmfully affected so many lives. In this book I'm not even going to try to untangle the bizarre and confusing financial instruments and market imbalance that brought our country to this pass.

Having been a real estate broker for the last 20 years, I have seen previous recessions, sky high interest rates and dot com meltdowns, even the housing crises of the early nineties. But throughout it all, I have been able to continue to buy and sell real estate using the techniques that I describe here. Over time I've learned some good ideas for achieving home ownership even in the worst of times and I want to share them with you.

CHAPTER ONE

REAL ESTATE 101

I'll get into alternative financing ideas in the coming chapters, but first it is important for you to understand the language and terms that are used in the world of real estate.

Seller's Market:

There are a number of basic things you need to know before buying a house. First off, the real estate market is always fluctuating. Sometimes the market is "strong" in that there are more buyers than there are sellers. Houses sell easily in this market and sellers can usually get what they want for their property. This is called a "seller's market."

Buyer's Market:

When the market is "weak," there are more sellers than buyers. The sellers are more eager to find a buyer. The seller has a lot of competition for his property. Here the buyer is in the driver's seat. This is called a "buyer's market."

Right now we are in a very strong buyer's market. There are very few buyers for all the houses on the market. Any buyer out there is in position to get a great deal on a house. This has driven house prices down throughout the country.

It seems that there are several reasons for this down market. One is the high unemployment rate. Second, the high foreclosure rate and third, what I think is the main reason, is the lack of mortgage lending from banks and other traditional lenders. When there are no loans available, the buyers can't buy.

So bank policies have a huge impact on the real estate market. In my opinion, they are the main perpetrators of the recession. The real estate market will not recover until they change their practices. For the country to fully recover, the real estate market needs to be strengthened.

But not to despair. All these factors give you a great opportunity to get into a house at the lowest possible price, with the best possible terms. As a home buyer, you are in a very strong position to bargain with the seller to get what you want.

Asking price / Offer:

When you see a house listed for sale, the price listed is called the "asking price." Because we are in a buyer's market, this price is only what the seller is hoping to get for his house. You are expected to make an "offer." This offer will, of course, be less that the asking price. And the offer will include the kind of terms necessary for you to buy the house without a bank. We'll discuss in length these terms in the following chapters.

Down payment / Financing:

Buying a house, will typically involve what are called the "down payment" and "financing." The down payment is the amount of cash that a buyer is providing. The financing is whatever real estate loan or loans the buyer can come up with. The total of the down payment and the financing should equal the purchase price of the house.

Carrying:

If you were to have the seller take the place of the bank and provide financing, then he would "carry a note." "Carry" is a term often used in the real estate business. It is what a person does when they provide a loan to you to enable you to purchase a property.

The Note / Holding:

The "note" is the contract paper that says you promise to pay back the loan under certain terms, at a certain interest for a certain period of time. The seller or whoever, could also be said to be "holding" a note. Holding here means just about the same as carrying, only sometimes it refers to a third party who isn't the seller, maybe a private investor.

Escrow:

In some states, such as California, the real estate transaction is handled by what is called an "escrow." Escrow companies are a neutral third party. That means they do not represent either the buyer or the seller. All contracts and money are given to the escrow agent who holds these items for the time specified in the purchase contract. At the end of the escrow period, the escrow will distribute the money as specified, giving some to the seller, paying off the old mortgage, paying any outstanding property taxes, title company fees, etc. The escrow will create all the necessary documents and deeds and see that they are filed with the County Recorder. This establishes your legal rights to the property.

Some parts of the U.S. don't use escrow companies. In that case, both the buyer and seller have to hire lawyers to represent them in the purchase process. For the most part, lawyers handle everything in much the same way an escrow company does. In this book I may refer to a transaction being handled by an escrow, but it will also apply the same way if lawyers are involved.

Title:

A title company will also be involved with the transaction. The escrow company or lawyers handle all coordination with them. "Title" means a claim or a right of ownership to real estate. A title company's main purpose is to guarantee a "clear title" to the buyer. They issue what is called a "Title Insurance Policy" to the buyer. This gives the buyers the security of knowing that the property they have purchased is free of any claims by an outside party. In my part of the country the seller usually pays for the title insurance. The escrow fees are split between the buyer and seller, but this may be different in your area.

In the old days before title insurance, a property could change hands without any guarantee that the buyer was getting what he thought he was purchasing. There were even cases of sellers selling the same property to more than one party or selling property they didn't even own. There were also many disagreements over property boundaries.

The title company will write you a "title insurance policy" that guarantees you complete ownership as well as exactly specified property boundaries. If any problem arises with the title after the closing of escrow, then the title company will have to resolve the problem or refund the purchase price.

The recording:

When you buy a home you are given a deed to the property. You might ask: "Where does that deed go?

What is my proof that I really own this house? How am I protected from someone else claiming ownership?"

The answer is that your deed is recorded at the County Recorder. This is an office that was created for just this purpose. It has been authorized by state law to record deeds, mortgages, easements, contracts for sale, court judgements and any tax liens. Actually the recorder will record any transaction that affects the title to the land.

You can imagine the chaos if there were no central location for people to record their ownership rights. In ancient days all the land was owned by the king and he would give land charters to his barons. Most everyone else was a land tenant (renter). When towns started to form the local lord might sell land deeds to the merchants, churches etc. He might keep a copy of this document in his castle for his records.

In parts of the U.S. during the nineteenth century, land was first owned by the Federal Government and grants were given to individuals for homesteading, prospecting, etc. States also owned great portions of land and they would also issue grants. In the Southwest grants were originally issued by the Spanish Crown. Some of these were sold to Yankees, some were stolen, and some continued to be held by Mexican Dons (titled Mexican nobility).

The County recorder is where the title company goes to research the title on a property. They must establish what is called a "chain of title." This is a recorded history of events that affected the title to that property beginning with the original land grant.

Another interesting bit of information about recording deeds is in the following example: Say an unscrupulous property owner granted the deed to his property in two separate card games to two separate people and these guys didn't bother worrying about title insurance. Well who owns the land? You'd think that it would be the guy who received the title first. But not so. The land belongs to the person who records the deed first.

Equity:

Here is a word that will come up often when dealing with real estate. "Equity" means the same thing as the cash value of your property. It refers to the amount of value that is in a house after you subtract the mortgage debt.

For example: You own a house that cost you $100,000. You have a mortgage amount of $80,000. The remaining $20,000 is the cash value that you have left. The $20,000 is the equity you have in your house. If you sold the house in most instances, the equity would be the cash you retain.

Encumber:

When you have a mortgage on your house, it is said to "encumber" the property. The mortgage is an "encumbrance." The dictionary says that to encumber is "to hold back or to burden." I guess you could say that a mortgage is a burden on a property.

There are other types of encumbrances that can be recorded such as tax liens, CC&R's (conditions, covenants, and restrictions), mechanic's liens or unsatisfied judgments. There are encumbrances against a property that aren't recorded. These include zoning laws, building restrictions, property taxes and special assessments. There seem to be a lot of things that can attach themselves to your property.

First and second mortgage:

When you hear people talk of holding a "first mortgage" on a house, they are referring to the fact that their mortgage is in first place. This means that their mortgage for a particular property was recorded at an earlier time and date than any other mortgage. Any mortgage recorded after that time and date will take a second position. It will be called a "second."

The reason that these numbers are important is that if a property were to be foreclosed on, the first mortgage would get paid first. Only then would the second mortgage get paid. There can be a series of mortgages, a third, a fourth, etc. But each one will only get paid after the one in front of it. If there is not enough money left, then the second, third or fourth mortgage will not get paid.

In a foreclosure, it is not that uncommon for a second mortgage to be left unpaid. That is why in a market like this, banks have just about stopped giving seconds. They use to call them equity loans or equity seconds. When the market was hot, equity loans were easy to get.

But with excessive foreclosures of today's market, these loans turned into a bad risk for banks.

Trust Deeds:

In some parts of the country, "trust deeds" are used instead of the traditional mortgage. In those areas you will hear real estate people talk of a first or second trust deed. The difference between a trust deed and a mortgage is that in a trust deed, a third party holds the note and the foreclosure process is simpler, but takes longer. I could expand on this, but it isn't that important for our purposes here. The state you are in will either have mortgages or trust deeds.

Principle and Interest:

For our purposes here, "Principle" is defined as the amount of money that you owe a lender not counting interest or any fees. You'll often hear loan people talk about the amount of principle owed on a loan. Monthly loan payments will often include both principle and interest. That means part of the payment goes to paying down the principle and part to paying the interest.

"Interest" should be a familiar term to most of us. When we get a loan of any kind, the lender charges us interest. This is the cost of borrowing money. It is most often stated as an annual percentage rate. When a real estate lender says that he is charging five percent interest on a $100,000 loan, he means that he is charging five percent of $100,000 which equals $5,000 for every year of the loan. In ten years he will have charged $50,000.

Collateral:

The greater the risk to the lender, the higher the interest rate. Credit cards can have high interest because the lender perceives a high risk. These are loans that have no "collateral." That is they have no solid asset to back up the loan. A real estate loan has the property as collateral. If the loan goes bad, the lender can take the property. That is why real estate loans have lower interest rates. There is security there for the lender.

Amortization:

Here is an interesting word. You see it in relation to mortgages. You might hear real estate agents say that the loan is "amortized" for thirty years. What they mean is that the loan is structured to be paid off completely in thirty years through monthly loan payments. No additional amount would be due at the end of the loan period.

The way an amortized loan is put together involves a complicated bit of arithmetic. The monthly payment you make has both the interest and principal built into it. In a fixed rate loan the amount of the mortgage payment remains the same every month. It is constant. But the amount of interest and principal that is being paid each month is continuously changing.

In the early years of the loan you are paying mostly interest every month with a small amount of principal. As the loan "matures," the amount of interest that is being paid is less and the principal payment is greater. All this works out so that the loan is completely paid off at the end of the loan period.

Obviously the monthly payments are higher when you are paying off the interest and the principal, than if you were paying just the interest. Sometimes when loans are set up with sellers, just the interest payment is asked for in order to keep the monthly payment as low as possible. However, when the loan matures, the principle will still have to be paid.

Balloon payment:

No, this is not a payment for a kid's toy. It is actually a name for an inflated payment that sometimes occurs when the loan comes due and there is still money owed. The payment is a "balloon" in that it is much larger than the monthly payments have been. This problem of having a large sum of money due all at once, is the reason lenders came up with amortization. They would prefer that you pay off the loan in equal monthly payments.

Having a balloon payment come due is a hazard of short term, interest-only loans. These loans are often set up with a private party or a seller. Usually with such a loan, the borrower is anticipating getting the money from another source or reselling the house within the term limit of the loan so that a new buyer will pay it off.

The purchase contract:

The purchase contract may actually have several different names. In my area, real estate agents use a standard contract titled "California Residential Purchase Agreement and Joint Escrow Instructions." Rather long-winded, but it is specific to what is happening. There are also specific contracts for buying vacant land and for buying commercial property.

Each state or region should have their own purchase contract which complies with the required laws for that area. I suggest you look online. Usually you can download contracts for free, but sometimes you have to pay some small amount. On your search

engine, just type in the name of your state and the words: "real estate purchase contract." That should give you what you need.

The purchase contract will consist of a lot of language but will have places for you to fill in things such as the date, location and the address of the property you seek to buy. Here you will fill in the amount you are offering and the terms of proposed financing. These will be explained in more detail in coming chapters.

The deposit:

You will need to figure out how much of a deposit to offer. This is sometimes called a "good faith" deposit. It is different from the down payment. The deposit is given up-front when you make the offer. Its purpose is to convey the seriousness and sincerity of you, the buyer, making the purchase. The amount of the deposit can vary. There are no rules for this, but there are local customs.

Sometimes real estate agents may try to make you come up with a deposit equal to 3% of the purchase price. They might say that you need this amount to look like a sincere buyer. But this is a buyers market, the seller should be excited by any offer. So your deposit can be smaller, even as low as ½ % of the purchase price.

I have known of cases where buyers have used things other than money for the deposit. They have even written promissary notes or bartered items. In my opinion, it is preferable to stick with money to keep things uncomplicated. You will need to save your negotiating for the important terms you hope to get from the seller.

One thing to remember though, is that the deposit may not be refundable if you bail out of the deal at the last minute. In that case, it is necessary for you to have "contingencies" written into the contract to protect you from losing your deposit. I will discuss contract contingencies in a coming chapter.

Your deposit check can be made out to the escrow company or to a lawyer, not the seller. You don't want to hand the seller any money at this stage of the purchase. In fact, you never do hand him money, that is what the escrow company or lawyer are for. The seller doesn't get paid until all the terms of the contract are fulfilled and all the debts attached to the land are paid off.

CHAPTER TWO

HOME BUYING

Where to begin?

When you are making a home purchase, you would like it to be a fun and exciting experience. But there may be some unknown details and potential problems that might crop up. In this book I will try to anticipate those problems ahead of time and smooth out the process for you.

Because buying a home involves quite a few steps, you will want to have some help working your way through the details. Usually you will work with a Realtor, but there is always the "for sale by owner" situation that will require a bit of homework on your part. And I hope to help you here with that homework.

Your drive from work:

Lets start at the beginning, finding the right house for you in the right neighborhood. If you live in those parts of the country that require driving to work, the cost of gas these days may dictate how far you will want to drive. Driving time could be a strong indicator of where you will want to live. Start by acquiring a map of your area. A big fold-out map encompassing where you work and where you want to live would be good. Now mark the spot where your work is located. Now mark the main arteries coming away from that spot. Ideally you'll want to live within a half hour drive from work.

To figure out how far a half hour drive is depends on the type of roads leading from your work. If there are freeways or expressways close by, they may allow for greater distances – unless these arteries are always clogged during times when you would be using them. In any case you should drive on the various roads leading away from your business during the time of day you typically leave work. See how far you get in half an hour's drive time.

Your next step will be to circle those communities within the ideal driving range. These should be the places to start looking. However, if there are no desirable neighborhood within range, then you may have to extend your search outward.

If you are lucky enough to have public transportation available to your workplace, then where you pick up this transportation may be a major consideration as to where you will want to look for a house. You may want to have the transit station to be just within a short trip from your house. You can pick up a transit map and circle the stations that stop in neighborhoods you find appealing.

Neighborhood Amenities:

You will want to drive through the neighborhoods you've decided on and see which ones you feel comfortable in. Don't just look at the houses and trees. Do you have children? What is the school district like? Will your kids be walking to school or using the bus?

See if the neighborhood has other amenities that you find appealing. Do you like sidewalks and curbs or the more rustic feel of no curbs? Is the street full of parked cars? This is not usually the best sign. It may indicate overcrowding. But it all depends on the type of environment you're looking for. Some very desirable areas in some beach communities have crowded parking problems.

As you drive around, look to see how far the grocery and other stores are from the residential area. If you like peace and quiet, you don't want to live right next to a bustling commercial zone, but on the other hand you don't want to drive too far to go shopping either. Wouldn't it be ideal to be able to walk or ride a bike to the store? Especially if there were designated walking / riding paths.

With the higher costs of fuel and the emphasis on lowering emissions, you will probably want to plan on driving less in the future. Now that you are buying a new home, this is an ideal opportunity to plan for that future. To have a home that is convenient to your work and to shopping.

It is good to look for a community where you can comfortably walk the streets. I have lived in too many places where the streets are full of cars racing around. This is not the most ideal place to bring up children. You should be able to let your children out to play with their friends without worrying about speeding cars. A friend of mine told me that his kids never learned how to ride a bike because the street they lived on was too busy with fast moving cars. That is a shame. Every kid should experience riding a bike.

Solar panels:

Another consideration that is coming up more often these days, is the idea of eventually installing photovoltaic solar panels on your roof. These are the panels that produce electricity. They are pricey now, but the cost is coming down and they are starting programs where you can lease / option them for a cheaper price than you pay for summer electricity. I think they are going to be very popular in the future.

The reason I bring up solar panels at this stage is that panels work best if they are on a south facing roof. So if you have a choice between a number of houses that otherwise seem pretty much the same, try to go with one with the roof sloping south. Solar hot water panels are also becoming more popular and will require some roof consideration. But if a south facing roof just doesn't work out, solar panels can also be mounted on wooden platforms that can be erected in your backyard.

Location:

Anyone who has bought and sold properties knows that *where* you buy is the most important factor, even more important than *what* you buy. There is an old axiom in the real estate business. "What are the three most important considerations in looking for real estate?" The answer is: "location, location, location." This is emphasized by real estate professionals over and over. Where a property is located can be the main determinate of it's value. You can have a mansion located in an undesirable area and its value may be a fraction of that of a modest house in a desirable area.

Where you live will be subject to your work, but if you are between jobs or retiring, you may want to consider relocating to a more ideal location. Finding the right place for yourself and your family will depend on your priorities. But in any case, you will want to buy a house that will retain its value. And for this you will want to select an area that is growing.

Growth areas usually have new or expanding businesses providing jobs that attract home buyers. Watch out for those areas that are losing population due to a loss of industry and jobs. The best bet for finding properties where values are going to climb back up is to follow the movement of the population. The population seems to be gravitating to warmer more temperate regions of the country, this seems to be true especially for older people in their retirement years.

To repeat myself, a wise purchase in real estate should take into account your location. This is true in not only what part of the country you are in, but also what part of the city you are in. And with all the weather related disasters that have been in the news lately, it would be wise to avoid areas with a history of flooding, landslides, etc.

Home values:

You need to know how desirable your area is and you need to know the values in that area. You never want to buy the "best in the worst." That is, a very nice house in a very bad neighborhood. No matter how good and appealing the house may be, a shabby or troubled neighborhood will always bring down its value.

If you were to rent out the house, it would be hard to find good tenants willing to pay good rent if the neighbors are troublesome. In a good neighborhood, if you put in a little effort fixing a house up, it would be easy to rent and probably bring in a nice income with tenants willing to stay longer and pay more.

What may seem like an irresistibly cheap price for a house, may end up being rather costly if you haven't done your homework. Homework means knowing the area well before you even attempt to buy a property. You should be driving through the neighborhoods on weekends looking for "open house" signs. Look at the asking prices, see the quality of the houses — the size of the yards, etc. After exploring so many houses you will know when a real bargain comes up.

I can't repeat this often enough, when buying real estate, it is essential to do your homework. Research all the surrounding neighborhoods. Find out what houses are selling for currently and what they sold for last year.

Ask the real estate agents in your area, they should be glad to talk with you. If you don't know property values, you are just shooting in the dark.

Where to find home listings:

In the past, house listings were either found in the local newspaper or at a real estate office. Sometimes you could just drive the area you liked looking for "for sale" signs. But now everything is on the internet. Real estate agents will post all their listings on various "multiple listing" sites. These web sites have pages of house listings available to the public. They come with maps that will show you what neighborhood the house is in and usually a number of pictures of the outside and inside of the house.

Sometimes real estate agents will provide what are called virtual tours of the house. These will allow the potential buyer to navigate on the internet through the inside of the house and see views of every room. This really saves the home buyer time and energy.

Private parties who are selling their home without a real estate agent will often advertise on "Craigslist," the internet site that is free to advertisers. It is very popular with shoppers. There are a number of other internet classified locations that also carry homes for sale.

Using the internet allows you to review whole neighborhoods much faster than was possible even ten years ago. A lot of driving time can now be replaced by the internet. Everything you need to find out about houses for sale should be right there at your desk or on your laptop.

Finding a bargain:

The object of all your research in the real estate market is to be able to buy a house in a good neighborhood below market value. Look at your target area. Search for a house that is clearly below neighborhood values. When you find a property you want, work out a price you'll buy it for based on your research. It is a buyer's market. You should be offering below asking price.

It is better not to fall in love with a property too soon. Wait until you find out that you can actually buy it for a reasonable price and with good terms. If you can't get it for your price and terms, then you should think about moving on to another house. In this market you want get the best possible house for the best possible price.

Since you are trying to buy the property for as little as possible, you might want to look into what are called problem properties. These are properties that need fixing up, but they are in good neighborhoods.

Here the owner obviously has problems. And you want to be the problem solver. You can take that problem property off his hands (for a good discounted price). You can then fix it up and create a nice looking liveable home.

It is amazing what a little clean-up, paint and new carpet will do. One person's problem is now your opportunity. Most every problem has a solution if you are willing to go after it.

An easy fix:

As I have said, if you have the time and energy, it may well suit you to find a "fixer upper." You want a house that has "all the right things wrong with it." These are the best buys. Look for a house that has simple problems to solve, like needing paint, carpet, minor wall patching or a cleaned up yard. These are all relatively inexpensive to fix.

Avoid major problems like a cracked foundation, poor soil, bad plumbing, etc. These usually indicate too much expense to remedy.

So you are going to drive through what you have determined to be desirable neighborhoods, looking for a run-down house, in need of paint and in a general state of easily remedied disrepair. This is the perfect fixer upper because it is in a good neighborhood. And it should be the least expensive in the area. You want a house that will definitely be worth more when you fix it up.

A friend of mine was able to get a local youth group to inexpensively help paint, clean up and repair a fixer-upper he bought. Maybe you have family members willing to pitch in. They might even get their friends to help if you offer some cash incentive or take them all out for dinner. Whatever works.

Typically when purchasing a house, a buyer hires a "house inspector" to make a list of any problems and asks the seller to fix them. But it may work better for you in negotiations to fix the problems yourself in order to get a better deal from the seller in terms of price or financing. You will want to know what all the problems are before you finalize a purchase, so it would be a good idea to have a thorough inspection done.

House inspection services are usually reasonably priced and can save you a lot of money and headaches. You can find such services on the internet or yellow pages. Be sure to go with an established reputable company.

Forging ahead:

So by now you know that to get the best deals in real estate, you will want to have previewed many houses and learned the ins and outs of the real estate market you want to buy into.

To purchase a good property for a good price you have to get out there and be willing to make offers. Sometimes it takes a number of offers before the right one happens. Don't be discouraged if you can't make it work on a property, there are plenty of others to work on. But with every offer it is important to be optimistic. You want to feel you are presenting a good offer and that the seller will accept it.

In making an offer to a seller, be positive, expect a positive outcome. If you convey doubts about your offer, the seller will pick up on it and may be more likely to reject it. Being positive and optimistic about your success helps to break through any resistance you may encounter. Always be smiling when you present an offer. This will defuse the seller's reluctance. I have found that a positive attitude is infectious.

A review of the steps to take:

Now we can go through the steps of purchasing a home:
1. You decide what location you want to live in.
2. You drive through the neighborhood and check out the open houses.
3. You go on the internet to review all the house listings for that area.
4. You make a list of all the best possible houses for sale. Mark them on a map.
5. Call the sellers or the real estate agent and make an appointment to see the houses.
6. Go preview the houses you're interested in buying.
7. Decide on the best candidate.
8. Obtain a Real Estate Purchase Contract.
9. Fill out a contract with the price you are offering and the terms that you want. Take other blank contracts as the terms are likely to change with negotiations.
10. Call the seller or his agent and meet them at his house to present the offer.
11. Negotiate with the seller until you get the deal you want. This may take days and several phone calls and trips.
12. Once you and the seller have reached an agreement, write a deposit check (make it out to the Escrow or Title Company).
13. Now you take all the signed contracts and deposit check to Escrow or your lawyer.
14. Escrow or your lawyer will engage a title company to research the records of the property and

then prepare a preliminary title report for you to review.

15. You will need to arrange house inspections to see if there are termites or any hidden problems.

16. Escrow or the lawyers will write up the grant deed and other documents and have both the buyer and seller sign as may be required.

17. All the purchase money is put into escrow or given to the lawyer. This will come primarily from the "financing entity" (lender).

18. Once all the terms of the purchase contract are fulfilled and the time set for the escrow period has expired, then escrow or lawyer will deliver the signed deeds and purchase funds to the title company.

19. The title company records the deeds with the County Recorder and distributes the funds so that the transaction can close and the property is yours. Congratulations.

Tax shelter:

Owning a home can be an excellent tax shelter. This is because presently the IRS allows you to take the amount you pay in interest on your mortgage and subtract it from your taxable income. If you have a rental on the property then you are allowed to use what is called "depreciation." If you are renting out a portion of your property, then you may use that portion for depreciation.

The idea of depreciation is that as the building gets older, it is losing value as a structure. Sounds logical, but in reality many buildings just keep going up in value, no matter how old they are. It is because they are attached to land and over the long run land in growth areas goes up in value. The IRS only depreciates buildings (improvements), so that land is left out of the equation.

The IRS lets you subtract the depreciated value of rental property from your taxes whether it has actually depreciated or not. (These laws are up to the whim of Congress, so they may change).

The way depreciation works: Let's use a rental house as an example. Say you buy a rental house for $200,000. The appraiser determines that $90,000 is the land value and $110,000 is the value of the "improvements" (house, driveways, patios, landscaping, etc.).

The accountant then uses what is called a "straight-line depreciation" method. Presently the IRS is using the estimate of a 27.5 year life for the building. He then divides the $110,000 value by 27.5 years to get $4000. This is the amount that the IRS allows you to deduct from your taxable income each year for the next 27.5 years.

That is one reason that owning residential rental property is a good business. It is an ideal tax shelter. But what if you don't need a tax shelter? Then your rental property becomes a magnet for drawing in partners. These are people who generally don't have a lot of tax deductions in their normal business. They can bring some needed cash to the project in exchange for receiving the yearly tax deduction on the depreciation of this rental property. I'll be going into this in more detail in a coming chapter.

A residential rental building can be very attractive to investors who are in a high tax category such as doctors, dentists and lawyers etc. They can make excellent investor partners in your projects. They are often too busy in their own businesses to involve themselves in what you are doing. They're called passive investors.

Residential rental properties can make an excellent investment. The renter is buying your property for you. He pays the rent, which is paying your mortgage payment. You get an investment that is increasing in value and is a tax write-off. This has the potential of being an excellent money maker. Especially in the long run. I will go into more detail about rentals in a coming chapter.

CHAPTER THREE

SELLER FINANCING

Seller carry back:

The easiest way to buy a house if you want to avoid using bank financing, is one where the seller is willing to "carry back" some favorable financing. What this means is that you buy the house and the seller becomes the lender. You pay your monthly mortgage payment to him. This allows you to avoid having to deal with banks or other outside lenders.

The advantage of a carry back to a seller is that he now has an opportunity to earn a higher interest rate than is available for him elsewhere. These days he would find it difficult to earn even 5% on investments except in real estate. And because this property was his own house before he sold it to you, he can feel secure in the investment.

The worst case for the seller is that he would have to take the house back and re-sell it if you defaulted on your loan payments. But for his effort, he would be making extra money from your initial down payment.

A popular formula for seller financing is to look for a seller who owns their property outright. That is, they do not have any mortgage on it. This sometimes exists with older retired sellers or with people who have just inherited their deceased parent's house.

If they have to sell in a down market they may not be able to get a decent price for it. However both of you can benefit if you are able to offer a price they want, but with terms that you want.

Often when retired owners or inheritors are selling their homes it is because they want to get their equity out of it to live on. After selling the house they may not be interested in buying another house, they may just want to put the money into an investment that gives them a secure monthly income at the best interest they can get.

By carrying back a mortgage on a house the seller now has an advantage of a higher interest rate than they would receive if they were to invest the money elsewhere. And the house they have lived in is a secure known investment.

Terms:

Sometimes in trying to buy property, you may not be able to get the owner to budge on his price. But you may be able to gain an advantage if you can negotiate good terms for a carry back loan. This may be an important trade-off for you.

In real estate negotiations, terms are often more important than price. Some buyers are even willing to pay full price if they can receive very favorable terms. This still may be a good deal for the buyer, assuming he has done his homework and knows what the real value of this property is. Favorable terms sometimes include the seller carrying with a smaller down payment then you might normally have to pay.

Here is a example: Joe and Kate spent a good amount of time researching a neighborhood they really liked. They finally found a house that seemed to work well for them and their family. But they couldn't qualify for a bank loan. They approached the owner of the house to find out how flexible he was on his price. They presented all the arguments for why the house is priced above several others they saw and the foreclosure rate, etc.

However, the owner wasn't going to budge, he said he wasn't going the lower the price any more and that was that. They did ask the owner what he planned to do after he sold the house. He mentioned that he was not buying another house, but was going to live off investing the proceeds of the house sale.

Joe and Kate went home and did some more homework on the house. They realized that the price was actually good for that neighborhood. They worked out how much financing they would need. Joe's father had offered to lend them some cash to help with the down payment.

So after a few days, they returned to the seller with an offer to buy the house at his asking price if he would carry a mortgage on the house for ten years at 5% interest. They showed the seller how this would be a far better and more secure investment than what was being offered in the investment marketplace at this time.

After some negotiation, the seller agreed to carry the mortgage for eight years at 6% interest. Joe and Kate realized this was the best that they could get. And that they were now able to actually buy a good house in a good neighborhood without having to go to a bank.

No money down:

In negotiating a purchase, an experienced buyer can actually work out terms that can get him into a property with no cash down. There are multiple combinations of terms that he may use that can result in a "no money down" deal.

"Money down" is real estate terminology for the cash that is required for purchasing properties. A typical purchase requires you to put in so much cash and the bank or other type of lender puts in the remainder. Why would lenders give so much of the purchase price for a property? Because they consider land a secure investment, particularly in high growth areas.

It is times like these where the recession has created a strong buyers market, that it is possible to buy properties without using cash. This may sound impossible to many people, but it has been proven to work for some knowledgeable buyers.

There are many ways to structure no money down deals. The most typical is one where you assume the existing loan and the seller carries the remainder. You end up with a first and a second on the property.

As I mentioned before, older sellers often want to put the cash from the sale of their home into something that will earn them an income for their retirement years. What you are offering is a way for them to earn a steady income at a better interest rate than they might find elsewhere. Here their investment is secured by a property that they intimately know.

You may purchase this property with no money down by offering to buy it for the price they want if they carry back 100% of the purchase price. This may take some selling on your part. They will likely want to get to know you as an honest and sincere buyer. It may take time to build trust.

You can explain that their only alternative to your offer would be to discount the price and make less money on the sale. You can offer to have them carry for just five years which will give you time to sell or refinance in a more favorable market. You might mention that if they don't sell to you, they may not find another offer as good as this for a long time.

Another advantage for the seller is that he or she has the option of selling his mortgage note or trust deed to an outside party, usually a mortgage broker.

In this market, many sellers are getting anxious to sell their properties and don't want to face foreclosure or other ways out that will adversely affect their credit. The advantage for you is that you have just bought a property with no cash that you can live in and hold onto until the market goes back up and you sell it for a profit.

Wrapping the loan:

One technique that has worked well in the past is what is called a "wrap." The way it works: The seller's name remains on the original loan, he carries back a second and you pay him a single payment for both loans. In this way, you are "wrapping" both loans into a single transaction.

The seller may do this to get out of financial difficulties quickly and easily and it allows him to earn some interest income from your payment.

The draw-back with wraps is that many banks are writing clauses into their loan contracts that say that if the property ownership changes, then the loan is due and payable. This is called a "due-on-sale" clause. If the homeowner sells his house the mortgage must be paid off, unless the bank approves an assumption of the mortgage. Most often, however, qualifying for an assumption is the same as qualifying for a loan.

Contract Sale:

Here is a good solution to the wrap problem. The buyer obtains the property "on contract." Here the seller retains recorded ownership of the property and the buyer receives contractual ownership.

A contract sale is an idea that dates way back into history. It has also been called a "land sales contract" or "conditional sales contract." Here the seller retains legal ownership of the property until the contract is paid off either by monthly payments or as a result of the buyer selling it.

The buyer holds a contractual title or "equitable" title. That is, he acts as an owner of the property, but is limited by the contract. This is used when the buyer wants to assume an existing loan, but the bank has a due-on-sale clause. This contract may work very much like the "wrap," only here the seller retains ownership.

Using a contract sale allows the buyer to work with an existing mortgage and additional seller financing. The buyer otherwise acts as if the property is his in that he can sell it at any time. He is limited though, by not being able to add any additional financing outside of the contract he has with the seller. He could, however, work out an arrangement for a new loan that pays off the seller's contract thus ending their contractual relationship.

The advantage to the seller of using a land contract is that he retains the security of ownership of a property that he is very familiar with. As well he receives a monthly income at an interest rate higher than might otherwise be available to him. And these days sellers should be willing to work with any arrangement that will get the house sold.

Real Estate Agents:

There are many advantages to working with real estate agents. They should know their local market; what the values are and where to find good deals. But, some agents may steer you to a house that is their own listing, or a house that offers a better commission to them. They won't always necessarily show you the least expensive homes as their commission is a percentage of the selling price.

Before I became a real estate broker, I was looking for vacant lots. I saw a sign for some lots on a street. I called the real estate office to see what the asking price was. The real estate agent who answered told me those were not good lots, but he had much better lots available. I went along with him to see his lots. But I also pursued finding out what the selling price of the first lots were. As it turned out the first lot prices were far lower priced than those he was showing me.

For many years I was a builder. I knew what kind of land I could build on. The first lots were exactly what I wanted. I really had to struggle to get through the real estate agent to buy those lots. I found out later that the percentage of his commission on those lots was far less than those lots the agent was trying to get me to buy.

The motivation of that real estate agent was to obtain a bigger commission, not to get me the best deal. This particular event inspired me to get my real estate license so that I could find the least expensive properties myself.

My experience notwithstanding, another important service that an agent provides is in helping with contracts. They have access to all the necessary contracts for the purchase of a property. They know how to fill them out and help present the offer to the seller. As well, the real estate agent will help negotiate with the seller.

The benefit here is that some sellers feel more comfortable with an established real estate firm. The agent will also take the signed documents to the escrow or a real estate lawyer. From there the escrow or lawyer will do everything else.

The downside of working with real estate agents is that they may not want to engage in all the creative financial dealing that may be necessary to secure a good property without using conventional financing. And if you were to try to buy a property with the least money for a down payment the seller would still need money for the real estate agents' commissions.

Buying that employs creative financing usually works best with direct negotiations between the buyer and seller. There are some creative agents who could make it all work for you, but in my experience most real estate agents tend to be more conservative. However if the whole real estate process is really intimidating to you, then you should get help in whatever way you can.

Foreclosure Properties:

Houses that have been foreclosed on, are houses that the bank has taken ownership of. They are usually great deals in that the price will often be well below the going rate. But the problem for you is that the bank owns them and won't even look at an offer from a buyer who has not been pre-qualified by that bank or another bank. Usually there are no other financing arrangements they will look at, except all cash. However, you could bring in a partner who qualifies with a bank for a purchase loan. There is a chapter coming up on bringing in partners for a real estate purchase.

There may be opportunities to purchase while the house is in the process of being foreclosed on. The foreclosure process typically takes three to four months depending on which state you are in. A house that is about to be foreclosed on has a very motivated seller. Here you are dealing with an actual person not a bank. Now there may be an opportunity for you to step in and create a situation that will work for both of you. You can try the different formulas that are mentioned in this book, like working with a partner, using a land contract etc.

If the property is what they call "upside down" or "underwater," that is, it is now worth less than the mortgage amount, there is the opportunity to arrange what is called a "short sale." Here the existing mortgage holder (bank) is willing to allow the owner to sell the property for less than what is owed on it.

You can go to the seller's bank and negotiate the best price they will accept for a short sale. This may allow you to get the property far below its retail value. This means of course that the bank gets paid off at the close of escrow. Again, it may require a partner to qualify for a loan.

Buy the note:

Another interesting option that has become popular recently is going to the lender of a distressed underwater property and buying the note for that property. I know this may sound like rather complicated professional business for most of you, but it does work for those who have a bit more real estate experience.

If you recall, the note is basically the mortgage debt of the house. In this case the note is held by the bank and banks are used to selling notes, usually to each other. For a distressed property, the bank will be very anxious to unload the note at a discount. Their goal is to get it off their books.

Here is how it can be done. You find a distressed property for sale. Talk with the seller. Find out who the lender is and get the loan number. Call the bank and ask for the department that handles the selling of notes.

The bank department that handles selling notes is actually much more flexible than the short-sale department. You should be able to get a good discount on the note, sometimes up to 50% off the note's face value, which is the existing mortgage amount.

However, now you need to come up with the *cash* for buying the note. By negotiating with the bank up front, you found out the amount that you need to raise. If you have the cash, great, but if not, you need to find some investors.

Put together a cost analysis sheet showing the property's value, average neighborhood values, and the amount of the discounted note. Investors should be excited by a chance to take control of a property at a good discount.

Owning the note is just the first step. Your goal is to purchase the property. The next step is to go to the homeowner and offer to buy the property at a reduced price. Because you are now the mortgage holder, you have more flexibility in what price you are willing to pay. Be sure you are working with a homeowner who is eager to sell and not be foreclosed on.

Another option would be to ask the homeowner to do a "deed-in-lieu" of foreclosure. A deed-in-lieu is where the homeowner gives the lender or note holder the deed allowing him to walk away from the house. He knows that the property is worth less than the mortgage, and may be anxious to get away from this debt.

Usually a bank will report this to the credit bureau, but you can create a more comfortable situation for the seller by you not reporting the deed-in-lieu to the credit bureau. Now you have the option of either moving into a bargain home or making some money by selling the house at its full value on the open market.

For sale by owner:

Perhaps the best way to find bargain real estate is to find sellers listing their own properties. These are found with "For Sale By Owner" signs in front yards or on the internet on Craigslist, or a number of other online or newspaper classifieds that are out there.

The most flexible sellers are usually ones with a problem. A problem that you can solve for them. Here are some typical sellers' problems that would make them want to sell their properties quickly:

1. The seller is in bad financial straights. He has enough equity in the property so a short sale doesn't make sense, he might be willing to trade for something of value, rather than lose his property to foreclosure. See my section on bartering.

2. A seller may have a rental property that has a high negative cash flow. If you are buying it with

the idea of keeping it as a rental property, then you may have an investor partner who doesn't mind the negative cash flow. He may need the tax write-off.

Other options are that you may be able to refinance the property at a lower rate to reduce the negative. With some improvements to the property, you may also be able to raise the rents on the tenants depending on their rental contract. Sometimes older landlords keep rents the same year after year and never raise them even when there is a negative cash flow on the property.

3. Some sellers are drowning in credit card and other debts and just want to liquidate their property as soon as possible.

4. Sellers may have just inherited a property and are anxious to get their money out of it. These sellers may also be interested in carrying back a mortgage and getting a monthly income. Probate sales can be a good place to find a bargain, especially if you are able to buy early in the probate proceedings before the competition arrives. Again, you might try the internet.

5. Sellers with medical problems and medical bills piling up may be anxious to sell. You may be doing them a service, allowing them to get out of the property now, rather than having to face a long drawn out wait for another buyer.

6. Sellers in a divorce may need to sell their old house right away to divide up the proceeds.

7. Other emotionally motivated sellers are business partners who are breaking up. They may

want to liquidate their rental properties as fast as possible. Partners sometimes expect too much from a partnership and if things aren't exactly as planned, then they want to get out quickly.

8. A job transfer may inspire a seller to discount his house just so he can move on.

9. Some sellers just aren't suited to the time and effort involved in managing rentals. This may be particularly true if the seller lives too far away from his rentals. Instead of hiring a management company, he may just want be free of the responsibility.

All of the sellers mentioned above have a strong motivation to sell their property and should be open to your creative financing ideas.

Working with a seller:

A difficult or temperamental seller is a more challenging barrier to buying a house than any problems with the property. If you run into such a seller, it is better not to bother. For the best deals, you need a cooperative seller who is willing to work with you.

Before you present an offer to a seller, do your homework. Be prepared. Get to know the neighborhood and its values. You should know what the best price is for your offer. And if it is a down market, you need to keep up with the latest prices. You should know how many foreclosed properties there are in the area.

When you meet with a seller, you will want to have all your figures ready. Because we are presently in a recessed real estate market, it may be necessary for you to educate the seller on the realities of the market. But remember to be courteous.

Since you have done your homework and will know the numbers in your area, you can give the seller the following points. Fill in the numbers where I have put parentheses:

1. We are in a serious deflationary period that may last for years.
2. Just a few years ago the median price for a property in this town was $( ) and now it is $( ).
3. There are an average of ( ) properties on the market in this area each month with only ( ) selling at rock bottom prices and many of those were bank owned.
4. Currently there are over ( ) foreclosed properties in this town.
5. There is a "shadow inventory" of properties that banks have that are ready to be foreclosed upon. But the banks are keeping them off the books out of fear of devaluating an already battered market. Nevertheless, these properties will be hitting the market in the not too distant future.

Presenting an offer:

A good way to present an offer is to set up a meeting with the seller at the house that is for sale. If you think you may have difficulty dealing with a seller, you might want to bring along a friend or relative who has more negotiating skills. If there is a real estate agent involved, he or she should be there.

In any case, be sure to have the purchase contract with you. I recommend bringing a couple extra blank contracts with you in case you are able to negotiate alternate terms. But keep them in a folder or a briefcase.

If you feel the house is overpriced, you will want to lower the seller's expectation of profit. In addition to the points listed above, you may also use the following technique. Try asking questions such as:

1. Is there mold or dry rot?
2. Does the roof leak?
3. How old is the plumbing?
4. Have there been a lot of animals in the house?
5. Do people smoke here?
6. How long has the house been on the market?

Try to be tactful, but don't be afraid of acting as if you're not quite sure you want the property. But there is a delicate balance between looking disinterested and alienating the seller. There are cases where a hard nosed buyer just angers the seller. My wife and I once sold a property for a lower price to people we found very nice and courteous, rather than getting more money from really obnoxious people who had made a higher offer.

The other extreme doesn't work either. We use the term "fish" for people who go through a house naively saying things like; "This is the only house we can find that we like." or "This price seems so cheap." In other words, such buyers are already caught – hook, line and sinker. All hopes of negotiating a lower price are gone.

If you are trying to buy below the seller's asking price, you will want to create greater flexibility in the seller's mind as to the house's value. Another technique is to talk about other properties you are looking at. You can compare the house size, number of bedrooms and baths and the price. Maybe you've seen another property at the same price but it is larger or in a better neighborhood.

An old salesman's trick is to steer the sellers toward the kitchen table. The theory is that they tend to make their decisions there. Politely re-ask some of the questions concerning the condition of the house.

In the negotiations, you are not just looking for a low price, but since you are trying to buy without a bank loan, you need to talk about terms. One way to bring up this subject is to ask the seller: "Why are you selling?" The answer he gives you may open up a whole new strategy for you. He may want to take the sale proceeds and put them in an investment for a steady income. If that were the case, you could describe how much better it would be for him to carry the mortgage on the house. He could earn a good interest rate and would be comfortable with carrying a note on property that he is very familiar with.

Remember, before you do a final negotiation on a price for the house, you will want to have figured out all the financing. If you are using the seller to finance the purchase, you will want to take this into consideration. In this case, the terms of the sale can be more important to you then the actual price.

You could tell the seller that you may be willing to meet his price, but only if the seller is willing to give you favorable terms. Sellers will often give better terms in exchange for a better price. It may be an advantage to you not to push the seller for the lowest possible price if he or she is willing to finance. This works well with a seller who is not flexible on his price.

If, on the other hand, you have another outside source of financing and are not in need of terms from the seller, then you will want to try to get the best possible price for the house.

One technique to expedite the sale and help you establish his best price, is to ask the seller if he were to commit to a deal immediately, what would be the rock bottom price he would accept. It is important to get the seller to commit to a price before you do. Ask again if you have to, then be silent. When the seller gives you a price, you might remain silent for a moment or two as if quietly mulling it over. During this time you might also read over the list of answers that you have been given as to the problems the house has.

This delaying process may cause the seller to offer a lower price. But stay silent – that is what works best. Once again be silent as you assess the new price. Then write down an amount you are prepared to offer in your notebook. Show the number to the seller, and explain that this is the highest you can offer due to the condition of the house and the neighborhood values.

When you have finally reached an agreement, if it varies from the contract you already have written up, then pull out on of the blank contracts you brought with you. Now you can start filling it out so you can get signatures right there and then. As I stated earlier, there are many good real estate contracts available on-line and the contract you use should be specific to your state.

Contingencies:

Most good contracts will have "contingency" clauses already printed up in them. If not, you will need to write them into the contract you use for the sale. Contracts should have blank spaces for this purpose.

Contingencies are important for a buyer. Their purpose is to provide you with a way of cancelling the sale without any penalties, such as losing your deposit. They allow you a way out of the deal within so many days if it doesn't look like it will work for you.

Contingencies can be for just about anything. Typical ones are loan contingencies. In a case where you are having to obtain outside financing from a partner or other private lender, you will want to add a contingency that you are able to get the necessary funds you need for the purchase. This clause says that if you can't get a loan within so many days, then the contract is cancelled. You could also have a contingency that your partner or investor approve of the purchase.

Property boundaries:

Property boundaries are also a common contingency. You can state that the seller will provide survey stakes at the property corners for the buyer to inspect and approve. This can be more important than you would think, particularly if the seller has a contentious relationship with his neighbor.

If the property corner markers have disappeared then the seller may have to hire a surveyor to find the original location of the markers. One mistake many people make is to assume that the existing fence is on the legal boundary of a property.

My wife's parents purchased a home that had a fence more than four feet inside their property line. The neighbor next door was in the process of building his home, when my wife's parents obtained a professional boundary survey and discovered the discrepancy. If the neighbor had bothered to do his homework (due diligence), he wouldn't have gotten stuck with a very abbreviated driveway when my wife's parents moved the fence over to the legal boundary.

Preliminary Title Report:

Another important contingency you may want to put into the contract is your approval of the "preliminary title report." The title company will prepare this usually within a week or two of opening escrow. It is a document that you should review to make sure there are no problems with the property.

Be sure to look out for what are called CC&R's. These are "covenants, conditions and restrictions." If they show up on a property, then you must read them carefully. They can greatly restrict what can be done on a property. They can inhibit certain pets, dictate the color of your house, prohibit parking RV's in or around your house, control any house additions or landscaping and possibly present many other prohibitions. If the CC&R's are too much for you, then you can use this contingency to get out of the purchase with your deposit.

Termite Inspection:

You will want to have a contingency for termite inspection. Here it is common to hire a termite company to do a house inspection. Usually the seller pays for this service. The inspector will issue a report and you can decide if you want to have the seller pay for any required repairs. If the repairs are too extensive and the seller won't pay, then you might want to back out of the sale using this contingency.

House Inspection:

A house inspection is similar to a termite inspection. A house inspection company is hired, but this time the buyer usually pays for the inspection. The inspector will create a list of any problems and defects he may find and again you decide if you want to have the seller be responsible for having them fixed. If you can't come to an agreement, then you have the option of walking away. However, if the problems are minor, then you may want to use them to negotiate for better terms or a lower price. You can tell the seller that you'll take care of all the repairs if he will agree to your financing proposal.

Most contingencies are time sensitive so you'll need to get all the inspections taken care of within the time period stated in the contract.

Without contingencies the seller could keep your deposit money if you have to back out of the purchase. It is not uncommon to have a property in escrow and then discover that it is not the deal you were hoping for. With the right contingencies written into the purchase contract, you simply inform the seller that because of a particular contingency you will not be able to complete the purchase and by law he will have to release the deposit.

Best way to buy:

To have a seller carry back a significant portion of the financing is by far the best way to buy your home. Seller financing should provide a much better deal for you than if you had bank financing. With seller financing you won't have to face the difficult qualifying requirements or those high loan-origination fees that banks demand.

In using seller financing there are advantages for the seller as well. If he receives all the funds at the close of the sale, then he may be faced with income taxes on that amount. But when he carries back a note, he doesn't receive all the money at once. His tax liability for that year is limited to the amount he receives in that year. It may be advantageous to him to have his profits spread out over many years with an "installment sale"– which is another way of saying that he is carrying back the mortgage.

Another advantage would be for some older sellers who want to set up a steady income with the money they receive from the sale. By carrying back a loan on the house, often the seller will be receiving a much higher interest rate than could be found elsewhere. Bank savings accounts are a offering very low interest rates these days and CD's aren't much better. In my opinion, the stock market has become far too risky. Real estate is one place where a seller can earn a decent interest rate and since he is familiar with the property, there is some level of security.

Seller gets you a bank loan:

Sometimes you may find a seller who owns his house free and clear or has a very low mortgage on it. But he doesn't want to carry a note, he needs cash *now*. You want to buy his house, but you can't qualify with a bank.

Here is one solution that has been used from time to time. Often an older seller who owes very little or nothing on his house will be able to qualify for a new bank mortgage loan. His house has plenty of equity and lenders like this type of borrower.

Since he is eager to sell and you are the only buyer he has, you could ask him if he would get a new bank mortgage loan for the house for the maximum the bank will lend. After he acquires the loan, you can then buy the house with a wrap or contract sale as I described earlier. You are then taking over the responsibility of the new loan payments as you move into your new home. This gives him the money he needs and you the house you want.

Seller gets a second:

A variation of this arrangement would be if you wanted to wrap his existing financing but don't have enough cash for the down payment. The seller could get a second trust deed on his property. You could wrap or contract sale both the first and second mortgages into one monthly payment. In this situation you would be making a single monthly payment to the seller. One problem here is that few banks at this time are offering second mortgages. These were very popular years ago and I'm hoping they will make a comeback in the years to come.

CHAPTER FOUR

OTHER FINANCING STRATEGIES

Private lenders:

There is a whole network of private lenders that will make loans on real estate in the same way that banks do. Only these lenders typically will require just the equity in the property as a basis for the loan. That means they do not have to look at your personal qualifications. Your credit score and your employment should not come into question.

Private lenders are called "hard" money lenders. That is, they lend only on "hard assets," the building and the land it is on. The reason that private lenders look only at the property as a basis for their loan is that they are charging a lot more interest than banks are.

A hard money loan these days can be as high as 11% interest. Even higher for greedy lenders.

Some private lenders want a lower LTV. LTV means "loan to value." And they may want to keep their loan to 70% LTV or lower. If a loan has a 70% LTV, that means that the loan is 70% of the property's value. If the property is worth or has a value of $100,000, then the loan would be for $70,000.

Private lenders specialize in loans to people who can't qualify for bank financing. They require that their loan be structured as a first mortgage. Because of all these factors, you will need to combine this private loan with other types of financing unless you have a large amount of cash to put into the purchase.

Points:

There are other costs that come with a hard money loan. The lender will charge "points." One point equals one percent of the total loan amount. Points are charged up front as a loan origination fee. Private lenders often charge 4 to 6 points for giving you a loan. Banks usually charge 1 to 3 points. Some unethical hard money lenders might try to get away with 10 or more points, but at such a high cost, it sounds like you're dealing with a loan shark.

Typically you would not have to actually pay the points out of your own pocket. The points would be included in the loan. Say you needed a loan of $50,000. Four points would equal $2,000. The amount of the actual loan would then be $52,000 and the lender would keep the $2000 for his trouble.

Loan broker:

Hard money loans are usually set up with specialty loan brokers and often a good portion of the points go to them as their commission. In my experience, they usually get the money they loan out from older retired individuals looking for a nice return on their savings. These brokers can be found on the internet by typing in the name of your state and the words "hard money lenders."

You might wonder why anyone would want to pay so much for a loan. A hard money loan, say 11% interest and 4 points can work for a short term loan if the potential profit on the deal is high enough. If you were buying a fixer and planing to work on it to increase its value and sell it within one year for a nice profit, the extra loan costs of a hard money loan may be acceptable.

Lets look at an example. If I buy a house for $60,000. The private lender gives me a 70% loan or $42,000 at 11% percent interest plus $1680 (4 points). I have enough cash for the 30% down payment. Now I fix up the place and increase its value to $100,000. After one year, I sell it for a profit of $40,000 minus $1,000 in estimated selling costs which are commissions and escrow fees. In the year I have owned the property, I paid $4,620 in interest and $1680 in points. Subtracting these from the profit and selling costs, I have a net profit of $32,700. Plus I was able to live in the house during this period.

Here are the figures:

- Purchase price ——————————— $60,000.
- Down payment ——————————— $18,000.
- Hard money financing ————————— $42,000.
- Sales price ———————————— $100,000.
- minus purchase cost ————————— $ 60,000.
- minus selling costs ————————— $ 1,000.

————————

- Gross profit ———————————— $39,000.
- minus one years interest — $ 4,620.
- minus points ———————————— $ 1,680.

————————

- Net profit ———————————— $32,700.

Subordination:

In the previous example I bought a house using a sizable down payment. In most cases you won't have that kind of cash lying around. Here is an idea of using a strategy called "subordination" that will provide the needed funding for this purchase.

To be subordinate is to be below another in rank or importance. Subordination in real estate is a term for taking one loan and subordinating it to another loan. That means the subordinate loan will take a secondary place to another loan that you'll be setting up. The other loan takes first place and the subordinate loan takes second place when recorded in the county recorder's office.

Subordination is often used when you are seeking seller financing, but you also need to acquire a new hard money loan. Because the hard money lender insists on being in first place, the seller's financing must take second place. You then need to ask the seller to subordinate his loan to the hard money loan.

In looking at the previous example, I used cash for the down payment, now I have the seller provide financing that will take the place of the down payment or a good part of it. The figures could look like this:

- Purchase price ————————————— $ 60,000.
- Hard money loan ————————————— $ 42,000.
- Seller's subordinated financing ——— $ 18,000.
- Cash down payment ————————————— $ 0

No money down:

Here you have a classic "no money down" purchase. You can move into the house without spending any cash, saving your money for house improvements. After one year, if you sell the house, you can walk away with a nice profit.

You might wonder why the seller, in this instance, would be willing to subordinate his loan. The answer is that usually you are not asking for a big loan from him. It can be a short term loan. You could ask him for a loan that is for two years or sooner, with no penalty to you if you pay it off sooner.

Since the loan is for a short time, you could offer the seller a higher interest rate than you normally would. He might jump at an offer of nine percent interest.

Another advantage of a hard money loan is that private lenders will usually allow subordinations. As long as the private lenders are in first place, they are not concerned with what comes after them. Generally banks would not allow this type of arrangement. They want to see a financial commitment from the borrower.

Bartering:

Basically, bartering is trading goods or services in place of paying money. It has been very popular for people to trade one property for another. But you can use almost anything in a trade; cars, boats, gemstones, artwork, antiques, etc.

Anything of value can be used in place of money for your down payment on a property, so long as the seller agrees. Years ago I received a nearly new Mercedes as a down payment on a house I was selling. I loved it and I still have that car. I once traded another car I had for a new roof job. Bartering is a wonderful option particularly if you are short on cash.

I knew of a fellow who's father was a gemstone dealer and could acquire his gemstones below wholesale. This guy was able to trade some stones at retail value for a down payment on a house. You never know what will appeal to a seller, particularly if he is eager to sell.

You can use a combination of these items to purchase a house. Say you have a car and some gemstones. The seller may very well be in need of a new car and his wife may enjoy some new jewelry. If you are able to assume his mortgage, you may be able to get into your new home without having to tap into your cash funds.

Trading properties:

As I mentioned earlier, you can trade one property for another. There are property trading exchanges that offer a list of other exchange properties and there are professionals that help handle these transactions. You could ask a local real estate agent if he or she knows of such an exchange that serves your area or look on the internet under "real estate exchanges."

Also, the IRS has a special procedure for property trades. They are called 1031 exchanges. The exchange must follow certain rules in order to qualify for a tax deferment. There should be a real estate agent, escrow agent or a real estate lawyer in your area who will know how to structure this kind of deal.

Bartering is older than money. Money, after all, is just a medium of exchange. People have always traded items they no longer needed or had a surplus of for items that they did need. You need a house and maybe the seller needs a boat.

When you meet with a seller, find out what he needs. Even if he says he just needs cash. Ask him how he plans to spend it. Maybe he does plan to buy a car or a boat. You may not have those but maybe you could buy one at a discount and trade it for full value. Say the seller always wanted a large sail boat. I have seen sailboats over 20 feet long selling for as little as $500 on ebay. Such a boat typically sells for over $8000. If you could pull it off, it would be a nice savings for you.

You may have seen advertisements for country acres in some far off area that are being sold at dirt cheap prices. These may not have access roads or utilities, but they are land. You could buy such a property wholesale and use it at retail value to trade for part of your home purchase. While this particular option is less commonly used, it may be more successful than trying to negotiate a lower price with the seller.

The idea is that you can use your creativity to solve the sellers problems with you spending a minimum of your cash. You want to use cash only as a last resort.

Bartering for services:

You don't just have to trade items for property. You can also trade your services. If you are an accountant, an architect, a carpenter, carpet layer, a lawyer etc., you can offer the seller your services for a given period of time or a particular job in exchange for part of the down payment.

If you were an accountant, you could offer to do the seller's income taxes and maybe bookkeeping for a year in exchange for so many dollars off the down payment.

The option:

What if you found a property that you felt was a good bargain but you are not ready to buy it at this time and the seller is in no particular hurry to sell. You could offer the seller an "option" to buy the property at a future time.

An option is a contract that allows you to keep an offer to purchase a property open for an extended period of time. Depending on how it is written, the contract may give you the right to buy, lease, sell, exchange or mortgage the seller's property. The option contract provides specific terms and conditions that must be met within a certain time period.

Say you meet a seller who has exactly what you want, but you are not quite ready to buy. You can pay him for an option to buy the house within the next three years for a specific price. For this option you must pay an option fee. This fee can start below $1000 and go anywhere up from there depending on the value of the house. If you decide not to take the option, the seller can keep this fee. If values go up within the next three years, you are ahead of the game.

You may wonder why a seller would be willing to delay the sale. It may be that he is sick of trying to sell it at this time and is planning to take it off the market anyway, but now he has a chance to put some extra cash in his pocket and have a buyer all lined up and waiting in the wings.

Some investors will tie up properties using an option, wait a few years and then sell the property for a profit. They time the closing of the sale with the date they are required to make good on the option, so they don't really have to put much, if any, money into the deal. Not a bad way of making money!

If you ever try this, be sure to list the property with a clause that says: "this sale is contingent on the seller acquiring clear title." This means that you have a contract to buy the property you are selling, but haven't yet completed the contract. I have heard of some fast and loose buyers using this clause to try to sell property that they have only recently tied up in escrow. I guess they figure they have the property under contract. In some states they would have to disclose what they are doing to all parties in both transactions.

Lease-option:

Now here is a variation on the option that is great way to buy a house if you are just starting out and haven't been able to raise a down payment. You lease the property with a contract that allows you to move into the house on a lease but also gives you the right to buy the house at a later date for a set price. You can even structure the option fee to be included as part of your lease payment.

The lease contract can also be structured to allow a portion of the lease payments to go toward the purchase price of the house. That way, when you are finally able to complete the option and buy the house, you have already paid the whole down payment or a good portion of it using a part of the monthly payments you made on the lease.

Here is an example:

A young couple with very little savings finds a nice house that is available to lease. They love the house and feel it would be ideal to own as their home. They approach the owner and ask him if he would be interested in a lease-option. After thinking about it for a while, the owner says: "Sure, depending on the offer."

The young couple hires a real estate agent to help determine the value of the house and to write up a lease-option proposal. They meet again with the owner and settle on a price and set the length of time of the option to be three years. They also settle other important details, such as: 1. The young couple will provide a non-refundable option fee of $500. 2. Twenty percent of the lease payment every month will go towards the future down payment of the purchase of the house. After three years they are able to buy the house with a good portion of the down payment already made.

In a lease-option arrangement there are no standard provisions. It can be very flexible. All parts of the agreement, the option fee, the length of the option period, etc., are negotiable. You can structure the contract any way that will work for you and the property owner.

Some owners actually advertise that they will do a lease-option. Try looking on Craigslist, or the newspaper classifieds. Owners who are anxious to be free of a property and have a vacant house are also good candidates.

Work Credit:

Here is another way of using the lease-option. You want to acquire a house that needs repair and the seller doesn't live there. The property is vacant as the seller has used it as an rental property. The renters have made a mess of it. You could offer to lease the house from the property owner with a lease option contract. While you are leasing the house, you could be working on it; fixing, cleaning, painting, etc. Your work is increasing the value of the house.

Now with all these improvements, the house should sell at a higher price. If you are so inclined, you could actually market the house while still leasing it. The way this works is that your for sale listing must state that the sale is contingent on you acquiring clear title to the property. You sell the property and during escrow the original seller is paid off and you walk away with a nice little profit for your efforts. This will give you more cash for a down payment on your next property purchase.

A vacant fixer-upper:

Let's look at an example: Jason found an old house in a good neighborhood that needed a lot of fixing and repair work. He noticed that the house was vacant and it wasn't listed for sale. He researched the county records for the name and phone number of the owner. He called the owner and asked if he could lease the house with a lease option.

Since the house was vacant and in bad condition, Jason asked for a low lease of just $500 per month which was far less than a house in that neighborhood would rent for. He explained to the owner that the low lease amount was because he planned to put in a lot of labor to fix the place up.

The owner didn't have a lot options as the building was vacant and in poor condition, so he agreed. Jason arranged a meeting at the house to discuss the details of the agreement. A lease option purchase price of $150,000 was negotiated with the owner. Jason had found the price to be well below the neighborhood values.

The lease option was to last three years, but the property could be purchased anytime sooner. Jason, who was handy with carpentry, painting and other trades, was going to fix up the place. Since the rent he negotiated was so low, he didn't try to get a partial down payment out of the lease.

After two years the house was in good condition with new paint, repaired siding and roof and nice landscaping. Jason then put the house on the market for $250,000 and sold it for $220,000. He was able to earn about $70,000 (minus sale costs and material costs) for his labor in fixing up the place. Plus he had an inexpensive place to live during that time.

Jason timed the sale of the house with the close of the lease option so that he would not have to come up with any purchase money. Now he had some cash from this sale to move on to another house purchase, eventually moving up to his dream house.

Owner incentive:

When looking for a lease option property, two things stand out that may be a clue as to the owner's willingness to accept a lease-option offer. The first is if the phone number on the add is way out of town. Out of town properties are difficult to manage and after a while the owner sometimes gets fed up and will gladly jump at an opportunity to unload it.

The second thing to look for is a vacant house. Few owners, even wealthy ones, want an empty house just sitting there. It can attract vandalism and it produces no rental income to make mortgage payments.

One advantage to the owner is that as future buyers of the home, you will be much more inclined to take good care it and even work on the yard for him. This can be presented to him as a strong plus for the lease-option alternative.

If you have some special skills, say you are a carpenter, painter or handyman, you might be able to negotiate an even better arrangement for yourself. If you agree to fix-up and repair the property, you should be able to increase the percentage of the lease payment that goes towards the future down payment. This could be as much as 50% or higher depending on how much work needs to be done.

When negotiating with an owner, try to remain flexible. If he or she is uncertain about any of your terms, back off. Ask them what they would suggest. The conversation should be harmonious and agreeable. After all, you want to create a successful outcome.

An advantage of a lease-option to you is that house prices in many areas are now at rock bottom so that they can only go up in the coming years. In popular areas the prices are already starting to rise. A lease-option allows you to reserve a house at today's prices, so that when you are ready to buy, you'll still get the best possible deal.

Try a larger building:

Say you run across a duplex or a small apartment building. You are feeling brave and confident. The owner is tired of his or her responsibilities, anxious and in need of good tenants. You could offer to lease-option the whole building. During the lease period you will live in one of the units, manage and sublease the rest of the building.

You are proposing to lease the whole building. You are taking over the burden of the owner's management problems. He or she no longer has to worry about vacancies. You are offering him or her financial security with a set monthly income. In exchange you would like the building lease to be lower than the total rental income. After all you will be working as a manager which normally gives you a discount on your rent.

You want to emphasize to the owner that by having you there he has the security of someone always looking after the place, solving the problems of the tenants and keeping the place full by finding new tenants. In exchange for all this, you are paying less than what he would receive if the building were always full. But he is receiving a guaranteed amount every month without all the hassle and problems that he has been facing. You want to be able to solve his problems and in turn receive a good arrangement that will allow you to purchase the building.

You want to negotiate with the owner to allow you to credit a big chunk of the monthly lease payment towards the purchase price. Don't say you're reducing the cost of the building, you are just prepaying the down payment. You want to assure him that you are buying the building in stages. Your first stage is to be paying the down payment over the length of the lease period.

If you run into any resistance from the owner, you could offer to raise the price of your offer. After all the terms in these deals are really more important than the price. In reality, the price is mitigated by the fact that you will be taking the down payment out of the monthly lease payments. You can afford to be flexible with the price if you get the terms you want.

You do the maintenance:

If you have the time, energy and skill, you can have a discussion with the property owner about having you do the maintenance on the building. This should allow you to negotiate a larger percentage of the lease going toward the down payment. This also gives you the opportunity to trade your services for part of the purchase price. This would apply to both a single family house and a multi-family building.

You can tell the owner that you will be keeping the building in very good condition. You can negotiate to do painting, both inside and outside. You will see to it that the plumbing or electrical are working well. You can keep the landscaping trimmed and watered.

Get some help:

If some of these tasks are too much for you, you could find a neighborhood kid that has some skills and hire him to take on some of these tasks. Young people leaving high school or college these days are facing high unemployment. Many would be happy for the work/income. You could try placing an add in the neighborhood paper. Some local markets have bulletin boards where you can post a "help wanted flyer."

Problems with plumbing and the electrical system may require the services of a handyman. But the costs of hiring help should be far less than the amount you are able to subtract from the lease that is going toward the down payment.

The owner should be interested in having all these responsibilities taken off his shoulders. This will make the whole arrangement much more favorable to him. Now he or she can sit back and not even have to think about this building, just collect the monthly lease payments from you. The idea of taking on the owner's headaches should give you a good negotiating position.

Extra Income:

One more idea: Say you are leasing a building that is in disrepair. If you are making improvements with paint and landscaping, you should be in a position to raise the rents, particularly on the new tenants coming in. You have already negotiated with the owner for a set lease amount for the whole building. Now with higher rents you are creating extra income for yourself.

Reverse Mortgage:

Imagine a house loan that you do not have to qualify for and you never have to make any payments on for the rest of your life, no matter how long you live.

If you are sixty two or older, you might seriously consider a reverse mortgage. They work best if you already own your home and have sufficient equity in it. But a reverse mortgage can also be used for purchasing a home.

Reverse mortgages were set up by Federal Housing Administration (FHA) to help seniors be able to stay in their homes. The government uses the term "Home Equity Conversion Mortgage" (HECM) to properly designate this type of loan.

How it works:

The way the loan works is as follows: A bank or private mortgage company sets up the loan using FHA insurance. The borrower(s) – either a single person or both husband and wife – must be at least sixty two years old. The loans are limited to paying up to $380,000 to $480,000 depending on the age of the borrower and the value of the house. The older you are the more you qualify for.

Another requirement is that the house must appraise for about $625,000 to receive the above amounts. If the appraisal is less, then the amount that is available is less. At age 62 the Lender /FHA will give you a cash amount equal to 61.9% of the appraised value. But at this time, the value of the house has an upper limit of $625,500. So a 62 year old will receive a maximum of $387,184.

However the FHA insurance payment and Lender fees will be subtracted from this amount.

This amount that the borrower receives can be used for anything. Typically it is used to pay off the existing mortgage, but if you own the house with a small mortgage or free and clear, then any money that exceeds the payoff can just be handed to you – cash in the pocket.

The most exciting thing about reverse mortgages is that you never have to make monthly mortgage payments on the house as long as you live, no matter how long you live. You must, however, stay in the house and pay the insurance and property taxes.

The FHA insurance offers a guarantee to the lender that they will not lose money on the transaction. For this guarantee they deduct from the loan about 3.5% as a mortgage insurance premium. The borrower doesn't need to come up with this money, as it is taken out of the loan.

Another requirement of these loans is that no other financing can ever be attached to the property. These are really meant for retired seniors on a fixed income. More information about reverse mortgages is given by professional counselors who are required by FHA to give you extensive details about these loans.

Buying with a reverse mortgage:

Lets look at an example of buying a house using a reverse mortgage:

Bob is sixty two. He was laid off from work and couldn't find a new job, so he decided to retire. His retirement income is low because his 401K was trashed in the recession. He would like to move to a warmer climate for his retirement years. He was successful in selling his house and now has about $50,000 to work with.

What should he do? His income is too low to afford mortgage or lease payments on any kind of decent home. He doesn't want to spend his last years living in an undesirable neighborhood. If he uses the $50,000 for lease payments it will be gone before too long.

The solution is a reverse mortgage loan (RVL). He first needs to calculate how much house he can afford to buy. If the lender will give him an RVL at 61.9% of the purchase price, then the math says his house price should not exceed $130,775.

Here is the math:
- Available cash = $50,000
- RVL rate = 61.9 %
- Maximum loan amount = $50,000 divided by 61.9% = $80,775
- Maximum house price = $50,000 + $80,775 = $130,775

There will be other costs, though, so it is best to work with a smaller number. Bob finds a nice house in Sun City for $125,000. The lender will put in about $76,000. Remember, Bob does not have to qualify for this loan. The lender does not need to look at his credit report or income verification. Bob puts in a down payment of $49,000. Now he owns a great retirement home that he can live in for the rest of his life without making any mortgage payments.

Long term strategy:

If you are young and starting out, you may go through a whole series of home purchases. Ideally, after each sale, you should have more and more cash to invest. Eventually you might have enough to purchase more than one property.

You should think of investing in residential rental property. I have a chapter coming up on investment properties. I recommend owning these properties for many reasons.

When I was younger, I started thinking about retirement. What was I going to do for income after I stopped working? I realized that both my grandmothers, who were widows, were living off income from rental properties. I thought that is what I should strive for, owning rental properties to give me a retirement income.

The idea of investing in rentals as a retirement strategy can potentially bring long term income. When the stock market recession turned people's 401Ks into mush, many older workers lost what was going to be their retirement nest egg. They now have to start over, saving and saving so that maybe someday they can retire. Because of the present uncertainty in the financial markets, I think that residential rental properties can be a smart investment in the long run.

CHAPTER FIVE

BRINGING IN A
PARTNER

Say you found that perfect property. A property that is
priced well below market value in a good neighborhood.
The sellers are willing to carry with a cash down payment.
You really want this property but your funds are tapped
out and the sellers insist on a cash down payment. What
do you do?

Here may be the perfect opportunity to bring in a
partner and create a "joint venture," sometimes called
a "co-venture." A joint venture is basically a relationship between two or more people who join together in
a partnership for a specific project or venture. Usually
the partnership only lasts as long as the project. When
the venture is completed, the partnership dissolves.

You only want to use partners when the opportunity
is really excellent – ie: a great house with the price well

below the market value. The house should be in a good neighborhood and may be a fixer.

The whole idea of using a partner is so that you can buy a house that otherwise would be beyond your means. You are offering the partner a part ownership which translates into an eventual share of the profits. You may be giving up part of the profits but you would not be able to buy the house in the first place without a partner. This is how much of the real estate world operates. A group of people pool their resources to buy into properties they would never be able to do on their own.

The partner can be a relative. Maybe you have a rich uncle who likes you. You can offer him a 50% partnership where both of you share ownership in a joint venture. He would be providing the cash down payment and you would be finding the property, researching home values and negotiating the purchase. As well you will be living in the house, paying the mortgage payment and providing any work and maintenance that needs to be done.

This idea would work best if you were not planning to hold the property for a long time. If the property were a fixer, then you could live there and fix it up and after a year or two sell it for a profit and make your uncle a happy camper. This should give you some cash in your pocket to allow you to go after another property, maybe this time without a partner.

OPM:

Another way real estate professionals talk about partnerships and investors is what they call "OPM." OPM means "other peoples money." This is used when you plan on purchasing rental properties or homes that you plan to resell quickly. To use a partnership or OPM allows you to do what you wouldn't otherwise be able to do. You can move forward with purchases that otherwise would have been beyond your reach. You can now afford what you couldn't afford before.

When a really incredible opportunity comes along, even in a down market, you may have to move fast to tie up that property. If you have a cash rich partner in mind, you can do it.

It can be far easier to create success in real estate when you have teamed up with partners. Going it alone is sometimes too difficult and too expensive. Most successful real estate entrepreneurs use OPM. They have their investors share the risk.

There are plenty of stories about buyers who can't close a deal because they just can't come up with enough money. With a joint venture partner the money is there. The good buys will not escape you.

There are many opportunities out there that will give you a nice profit, if you have the funds that allow you to jump right in. Once you get the knack of operating this way, you will find it hard to resist the temptation to buy more than one property. I'll talk more about investment properties in a coming chapter.

Contractual Partnerships:

For years "limited partnerships" were a staple for people getting together in a joint venture. The way a limited partnership is set up was ideal for many types of property purchases. The partnership has two main partners. One is the general or managing partner and the other is the limited partner. There can be any number of limited partners.

The general partner manages the project, that is you. The limited partner or partners put in the money. They are limited in that they have limited say in how the partnership is managed. They are passive investors. Their participation is limited by the "Limited Partnership Contract." You put the project together, manage it and they put up the money. You'll need a lawyer to write up the contract.

L.L.C.

In recent years LLC 's have become more popular. The LLC stands for "Limited Liability Company." The LLC is made up of "members," the managing member and the investing members. This was intended to work the same way as a Limited Partnership, only there was to be more liability protection for the investors. If the property ran into problems and there was a lawsuit, then the investors would be protected from liability. Well, after a few court trials, this proved not to be the case in some states. The investors were somewhat liable after all.

Regarding which is preferable a Limited Partnership or an LLC, you would have to ask your lawyer what he thinks would be best in your state.

For real liability protection where I live, I've been told that the partners would have to form an S-Corporation. But all such legal maneuvering is out of my expertise, so you would have to go to a lawyer.

One thing that all this talk of liability brings up is the idea of honesty and fair dealing. If you are open and willing to work honestly with the seller, you shouldn't have problems.

Any purchase you put together should be a win for all sides. You are helping the seller unload his property in a bad market and you are giving investors the opportunity to make a decent return on their money.

If there are just the two of you, yourself and a partner, you don't really have to form any of the above partnerships, you can just be what is called a "general partnership." This is the designation that is given (by default) to people working together. But you should have a written agreement that states clearly the responsibilities of both of you, profit sharing, etc.

A partner who qualifies for a loan:

You have just found the ideal property. It is in a great neighborhood and priced well below the average house value. But the seller won't carry and none of the other strategies are working. And you just don't qualify for a bank loan. You might try to find a partner who will allow you to use his ability to qualify to buy the house using a bank.

This is often done with close relatives. Parents may qualify for a purchase loan for their kid's first house. An older, well established brother or sister might also be willing to help.

The banks call this "co-signing" on a loan. The partner and you both sign on the loan. Often you will need to give the co-signer a stake in the property, such as a half ownership. Here you would have the deed written with both your name and the co-signer as joint tenants with equal ownership rights.

"Joint tenants" is a term used in the language of deeds. It means two or more people who share an ownership in a particular property. Generally it means that each has equal ownership rights. You see terms on a deed such as "husband and wife as joint tenants." More than two people can be joint tenants, all with equal shares.

Another idea would be to have the partner buy the house in his or her name and later they could deed a portion of it back to you. There may be a combination of incentives for them to do this. If it is not a close relative, the incentive could be a share of future profits when you sell the house after the market goes back up.

Another variation of this idea, is for the partner to buy the house and you lease the house from him. He could then use the property for a rental depreciation off his income taxes. You should have a contract drawn up ahead of time that clearly states what your relationship is and how the profits are to be divided once the house is sold.

Your part of the partnership involves finding the property, negotiating the purchase and taking care of the mortgage payment, insurance and taxes. As well, you'll be responsible for the maintenance and any fixing up the property may require.

Family Partners:

The best partners are those you already know and trust. Usually family members. They may have money in savings or CD's with a very low-yield. That is, the interest rate that they are receiving is pathetic. They may also be playing the stock market. This has become more and more risky these days and if they do make any money, it may not be as much as you are offering them.

If you were to write it out on paper, you could show them that even with a 4% rise in a property's value, they could be earning more for their money than many other investments. This is because the down payment is usually just 20% of the cost of a house.

Say the house cost $100,000. The down payment is $20,000. If the house value were to increase by 4%, the house would now be worth $104,000. The profit is $4000. If the cash amount invested is $20,000, then $4000 represents a 20% profit before paying commissions and sales costs. Though the market is still sluggish in many areas, some areas are already showing a rise of 4%.

Business Partners:

Outside of your family members, you may know of business and professional people who know you and would like to lend a hand. Doctors and dentists may have spare cash and be interested in partnering in real estate. They are often buying into partnerships that give them a real estate rental depreciation deduction that will help with their income taxes.

You may be able to structure a deal that allows them to buy a house and have you rent it back from them. Often when investing in properties people have to share the depreciation with other investors. With this arrangement, your investor will get full depreciation of the property.

You will need to structure the transaction so that you can share in the profits. Once again, this will involve writing up an agreement that designates responsibilities and gives you and your investor an agreed upon portion of the profits when you sell the house.

Your share of the profits is justifiable because of your contributions – you found an excellent property, priced well below market value. You negotiated the purchase. You are also doing all the maintenance and marketing. Your share of the profits may increase if you are contributing extra labor in repairs and improvements on the property.

Though the investor is the owner, you've structured the partnership so he or she can be a passive investor without all the usual responsibilities of ownership. Your investor is, though, receiving all the full depreciation on the property. Investors are looking for a tax depreciation and you are looking for a place to live that will give you some future profits you can take into your next house purchase.

A written prospectus:

A written what? How do I do such a thing? Calm down. A "prospectus" is really just a summary of what you plan to do and how you plan to do it. Yes, you can type one up or have it typed for you. Anytime you are approaching a potential partner you need to have one in hand.

You want to look and sound like you know what you're doing. An investor / partner will want to see figures – costs, gross profit, net profit, etc. So, you will need to do your research before preparing the prospectus.

Start by writing the prospectus in a rough outline. Describe the property you have found. Give details about the house and details about the excellent quality of the surrounding neighborhood. Write down the price of the house. How does it compare to the house values in the neighborhood? Once again, do your homework and research the area throughly.

You should have already talked to the seller, so state what terms he'll take for the purchase. Now state your plan for buying the property. The prospectus includes a "financial analysis." All that is, is you listing the numbers in the transaction. List the purchase price, the down payment, the cost of improvements and maintenance. How much is being financed? Is the owner carrying?

Now you need to state how much profit you expect to make. Say you plan to sell the property after fixing it up. Or are you just waiting for the market to return in a couple of years? What is the projected profit after the sale. There will be a gross profit, but you will need to list sales costs. These include escrow or lawyer fees, title company fees and a real estate agent's commission if there is one. Other expenses include the money that you put into improving the property.

I think you should be getting the hang of it. Just take your rough outline, clean it up, maybe reorganize the layout and type it up neatly. It should only be a single page. Be sure to write your name, address, phone number and email. Give the paper a title such as, "Allen Street Joint Venture Proposal." Of course you will include the specifics of the property, its address, town, etc. Now you look professional and the investor should be impressed.

A written agreement:

It is essential when forming a partnership to clarify exactly what your responsibilities and those of your partner will be. As well you will want to clarify how the profits will be divided. All this needs to be written into an agreement that is signed and dated by both parties. The prospectus can be included as an attachment to this agreement.

I've found that oral agreements usually don't work. After a number of months people tend to forget or misinterpret what was said. A written document will remind them of their responsibilities and especially what the profit sharing arrangement is.

When dealing with a family member or a good friend, the tendency is to just shake hands on the deal. Not so fast. Here it is equally important to write down exactly what is being agreed to. A written agreement will prevent misunderstandings in the future.

Some people can conveniently forget what was agreed to, especially when it comes to dividing profits. People have selective memories. They tend to remember what they want to remember. And you want to avoid hard feelings, especially with family members or friends.

You can write up this agreement yourself. State the names of both partners, the date, the location of the signing and list the responsibilities of both partners. Put in a projected time frame for when you expect to sell the property and how the profits are to be shared. You both must sign this document and write in a date. Copies should be made for both of you.

In the agreement you will want to go into some detail regarding the responsibilities of both you and your partner. Such things as who is doing the accounting, paying the bills and making the repairs need to be addressed. You will want to cover contingencies such as what happens when one partner needs to get out of the partnership early, due to unforseen events.

This is a legal contract, so if you feel uncertain, you would be wise to have a lawyer look at it. He may have suggestions on adding more details or clauses. If you use a lawyer, remember to add in the cost of lawyer's fees to your cost projections.

Equal partnerships:

In some partnerships you will want both you and your investor to be on equal footing. That is to say that the value of your research, planning and labor are equal to the value of the money your partner / investor is contributing. He puts in the money but remains a passive partner. You are the managing partner. You research and find the bargain property. You contribute the planning and energy to make it all happen. You are responsible for the project's success. It is important to clearly spell out in your agreement that this is an equal partnership.

In a relationship like this it is not necessary for you to have to put in your own money. I have run into potential partners who thought that I should be putting in an equal amount of cash for a half share of the profits. But they also expected me to do all the leg work as if my time and labor were worthless. You really don't want to waste time with such people.

However, there are also projects where the amount of money that your partner puts in is great enough so that you are willing to give him a much larger share of the future profits. For instance, if he were providing all the financing for the house purchase and all costs related to the property– improvements, etc.

A partner buys the house:

Another way to structure a partnership would be to have your partner buy the house outright using his or her cash and good credit. You can create a lease option to purchase the house at a later date, say three years. You both agree on a price you'll buy it for and put it all into a written contract.

You move into the house and make the lease payments and take care of all the maintenance, etc. The investor gets a full tax depreciation and you get a nice place to live.

After three years while you are still leasing the property, you list it for sale with a contingency of acquiring clear title. You are planning to sell the property for more than the lease option agreement. When it sells, you do what is called a double escrow. The investor partner transfers the property to you and you transfer it to the buyer, all on the same day. Escrow handles the transaction. The investor is guaranteed his asking price and you can now walk away with a little profit for your efforts.

Honest dealing:

You want to be straightforward and honest with your partner. Sometimes things don't work out the way you planned it. Tell your partner right away what is going on, even if it is bad news. Try to fix the problem as soon as you can. Don't let it drag on. Maybe the house has some defect that you missed.

Tell your partner what the options are for fixing it. If it was your fault and he has to put up more money to repair the problem, maybe you can offer to subtract that amount from your future profits. He should appreciate your honesty and willingness to flex. It is important to maintain an open and honest relationship both ways. You should expect the same from your investor. As I cautioned earlier, always know who you are dealing with.

Meeting a potential partner:

You have found an ideal property and researched its value. You have searched for someone who will be interested in investing in it. When you have a good candidate in mind, you should prepare your prospectus and set up the meeting in a friendly neutral environment. You could offer to take him or her out to lunch at a nicer restaurant where both of you can sit at a table and talk.

When you meet with your potential investment partner, you'll first want to determine if he or she might be someone you want to work with. If they feel right to you, go ahead and present the property you found and how with just the right amount of work it can be worth a lot more. You can describe the quality of the neighborhood. Hand them your prospectus. You might also explain how a passive partner might be able to achieve a desirable tax depreciation without any of the ownership headaches.

This is an excellent investment opportunity for an investor. You are providing a valuable opportunity that will profit both of you. You can mention that the investment is secure in that the investor will be the owner of a good property in a good neighborhood. You will take care of any problems and be a reliable renter who will maintain the property.

In this meeting you want to present yourself as positive and confident. You want to create the impression that you are a successful entrepreneur. A calm business-like manner is best. Prepare all of your cost/profit figures ahead of time.

You want to look professional. You don't normally have to wear a suit. A neutral color sports jacket and slacks – for a man or a woman – can make a good impression.

You are presenting your potential investor with a great opportunity. If he or she doesn't show interest, just thank him or her and move on. In my experience you will find the right partner at the right time.

Bad partners:

There are such things as bad partners. It may be better not to go into a partnership than to be stuck with someone who isn't compatible with you. You want to work with people you get along with. The biggest stress in any real estate transaction is not the property but the people. A problem partner is distrustful, nervous, suspicious and is constantly calling you with worries, concerns or demands. Try your best to get a feel of someone's personality before you commit to a joint venture.

You want a partner who is at least as positive as you are. If the potential partner can only give you negative feedback, then thank them for their time and move on.

Equity sharing:

A common way professionals in the business refer to using a partner is "equity sharing." This is when both you and your investor partner are planning to share in the profits of a house that you plan to purchase, and then sell at a future date. Both of you are planning to split the equity profits upon the sale.

As seen in previous examples, equity sharing is most often used when you can't come up with a down payment, so you bring in a partner who has the cash. In exchange you offer him part ownership in the property. When the property sells he or she will receive his or her investment back, plus half the profit.

Again, your contribution is that you have done all the research and leg work to find a good value. You have negotiated a good purchase agreement. Plus you will be making the monthly payments on the mortgage while you are living there. You will also be taking care of the maintenance.

Unless there is remodeling to be done, then these types of partnerships usually last about five years in theory. Ideally that would give the market plenty of time to rebound and increase the value of the property.

Advantages of equity sharing for the investor:

In a project where the investor puts in the money and you occupy the property there are a number of advantages for him:

1. He has a rental property that he can use for depreciation.

2. Because you are his partner, you will handle all the maintenance and repair work that may come up related to the property.

3. There will be a steady flow of rent payments that go directly to paying the mortgage (coming from you).

4. You will pay taxes and insurance and maintenance costs, so the investor won't have additional expenses to worry about.

5. The investor could comfortably live far away from the property because you are handling everything.

Investor gets interest:

The way to increase the investor's enthusiasm, is to offer him a minimum interest return on his money. You can structure the partnership contract so that he will receive 8% per annum interest on the cash he's putting in or half the profits, whichever is greater. That way he can feel confident that he will at least make some money on his investment.

There are investors who are perfectly happy to just be making interest on their investment and not having a split of the profit. You can offer them 9% to 11 % interest and a lot of investors would be glad to invest. Actually they are acting as private financing, so you can just write up a mortgage note, like you would with any private lender. Again, blank notes can be found online.

I personally liked having investors just earning an interest rate instead of sharing the profits. They are a lot more detached and in no particular hurry. I had an investor who acted as a lender on several of my projects, only in those days I had to pay him 15% interest. But properties were inflating then so there was money to be made.

He was happy with the arrangement and kept wanting to invest in more of my projects. Then finally I made a real mistake. I asked him if he wanted be an equity partner on some houses, that is share the profits instead of just giving a loan. That was a disaster. He fussed and fretted over every dime that was spent and the market was getting weak so it took longer to sell the houses than anticipated. There was still money to be made, but he suffered every inch of the way. When he was making a guaranteed interest, he was a happy camper, but he didn't have the stomach to be an equity partner.

A good opportunity:

Equity sharing is a valuable tool to allow just about anyone to buy into a house that they otherwise could never qualify for. With this technique the home buyer can have someone else either qualify for a loan and/or come up with the down payment.

With real estate market prices at their lowest level in years, this is a perfect time for want-to-be home owners to move forward and grab up that incredible bargain that they see down the street. Even if it is a foreclosure, with a qualified partner you can make the most of the best deals being offered out there.

In equity sharing, you are assuming that the price will go up in the future, so that there will be a profit to split down the road. That is why you want to get the best bargain possible. And the bargains are out there. An opportunity like this does not happen that often.

To be able to buy a house at the bottom of the market has been rare. But you need to strike while the iron is hot. The real estate market will go back up, eventually. Especially in areas that are recovering quickly.

The seller as a partner:

Say you are a handy person, able to fix and repair things. You're good at cleaning and painting. What if you find a seller who has a rental property that needs a great deal of fixing up and you aren't flush with cash at this time. You could propose a joint venture with the seller. The proposal would have the owner retain ownership of the house and you move in and work on all the repairs, paint, yard work etc.

When you have the place in good condition, you sell it with the owner and split the profits. The amount of the split will depend on the sale price and the amount of work you had to do. You could try to figure out the value of your work if you had hired professionals to do it. Then you need to take into consideration that since you are living in the house you're working on, you also received a free place to stay during this time.

You can write up all these ideas in a proposal prospectus so that the owner can clearly see what the advantages are. Once you come to an agreement, then write down your business relationship in a contract agreement like I mentioned earlier. Joint venturing with a seller has a lot of advantages for you. You can get into a property with no cost to you, you have a free place to stay and stand a good chance of making some money when it sells.

CHAPTER SIX

REAL ESTATE AS AN INVESTMENT

As I suggested earlier, buying residential properties to use for rental income can potentially be an excellent investment. A good rental property in a desirable are can be a steady source of income for the rest of your life. It is an ideal retirement nest egg.

Real estate ownership is often said to be the backbone of wealth. Unless you know of a pirates treasure hidden somewhere, it is difficult to have a secure foundation of wealth without owning real estate, especially residential rental properties. Historically real estate ownership has offered a basis of financial security that few other investments present.

As you have probably seen and heard in the daily news, many other types of investments can vanish overnight and become absolutely worthless, but land is solid and permanent. It can't go anywhere. It is always there. It's paper value can temporarily diminish, but over the long run desirable areas continue to appreciate.

There is always something that can be done with land. You can build your home on it. You can rent it out. You can even grow your food on it. In my opinion, land is valuable. Land is the basis of our society. The basis of a healthy economy.

Rental security:

These days we are very much aware of the fluctuations in the real estate market. When we buy a property, we want to feel that we are protected from any market down-turns. That is why it is good to set up a rental income that at the very least exceeds what you are paying to own the property. You want to have the rental payments you receive cover any mortgage payments. It would be even better if the rental income could cover the insurance, property tax and maintenance as well.

If you can buy the property at a low enough price, then covering the above expenses is possible. This is called a "positive" cash flow. That means there is no out-of-pocket cash that you have to come up with every month which would be called a "negative" cash flow.

Owning a property for the long term with a positive cash flow would allow you to ignore the fluctuations in the real estate market. This is because rents usually do not change with the ups and downs of the market. Rents tend to remain fairly stable. In fact, when the market is on a down-turn, as it is now, the rental market is strong.

All those people who moved out of home ownership are now needing a place to rent.

Even those people who bought rental properties at the height of the market in 2007, can still be in a good condition if they set up a positive cash flow. They are in a position to sit it out and wait until the market climbs back up.

Tenant buys it for you:

I believe that residential rental property, if in the right location, is the best investment you can make. And it is real. You can touch it, feel it, and enjoy looking at it. With a positive cash flow, you could say that the tenant is buying your rental property for you. If you own the property long enough, the tenant ends up completely paying off your mortgage.

Say you buy a property and are able to assume the mortgage and have the seller carry back a second. The mortgage has twenty years left on it, so you ask the seller for his second mortgage loan to be amortized for twenty years. After you close escrow, you may want to spruce up the property so that it attracts a tenant willing to pay more.

You will want to make sure that the property is vacant if you plan on doing improvements. In this case, it is common for the buyer to request in the purchase contract, that the seller have the property vacant before the close of escrow. If the tenant has an extended lease, then the seller may have to buy out his lease in order to get the tenant to vacate.

Wants you have made the improvements, you have now increased the value and appeal of the property. By this you are able to set the new rental payments at an amount equal to the mortgage payments on both the first and second. This is a good deal for you, so you decide to keep this rental property and take the tax depreciation off your taxes year after year.

You hold the property for twenty years and the tenants pay off the mortgage with their rent payments. Now it is time for you to retire and the rent payment has become your retirement income. What if you had several houses set up like this? That could be a good portion of the income you'd need for retirement.

There would be some ongoing expenses, such as property tax, insurance and maintenance. But these would be well worth handling in exchange for the security of a steady income. And once this income is set up, there is little that can threaten it. Unlike the stock market, rentals are consistent. They rarely if ever go down. Even in bad times the rental markets tend to stay about the same and over the years they go up – good times or bad times.

The Good Tenant:

To have success with your rental property it is important to have good tenants. They are the ones that pay on time at the beginning of the month. They are quiet, courteous and dependable. Such people do exist, and you can find them.

It is important if you are going to attract desirable tenants that you are providing the kind of place they will want to live in. I have discussed how important neighborhood location is. So you have that covered. Now the house itself should be in as good a condition as you can make it.

Look carefully at the house. Start on the outside. The landscaping should be trimmed and green. Clear out weeds and any dead shrubs. Sweep the walkways. The house itself should look like it was recently painted. Maybe it needs more trim paint around the windows and doors. The front door may need a new coat of paint.

Now lets look at the inside. The walls should have fresh paint or at least look clean as if they were just painted. It works best to use neutral colors. If you go with a particularly strong color, that may not be a favorite of the tenant you want. If you stay with neutrals, the tenant can accessorize in whatever colors they may like.

The floor should not have stained or worn carpet. Have the carpets professionally cleaned. Better yet, if you have the money, get rid of carpets altogether. Most carpets wear out fast with tenants. I found it best to put down floor tile. It lasts forever, particularly if you seal the grout. I learned that with a tile floor, I can allow tenants to have pets without the typical problem of a pet ruined carpet. Also, blinds are more durable than curtains.

Cabinets in the kitchen and bath will look clean and new if you use white or off-white paint. Women particularly respond to a light bright freshly painted kitchen. Dark wood cabinets can look dingy after a few years. Also, paint grade cabinets are much less expensive. The appliances should have a clean and new look, as should the counter tops. I have found that for tenants, none of these items have to be expensive or brand new. Just freshly cleaned or painted should make a good impression.

It may seem like I am being picky but if you want a good tenant, the house you're renting has to be appealing. With a good house and the right price you should be able to select a good tenant.

I have found that advertising in Craigslist brings a good selection of tenants to choose from. In Craigslist you can put in pictures of the house, both outside and inside and you can write up an appealing add describing everything desirable about your place, all at no cost.

Put in your phone number, not the address. You will want to screen potential tenants on the phone before they show up. Remember though, you cannot discriminate, but you can choose. You can specify such things as no smoking, pets or no pets and a quiet tenant. Usually just a phone conversation will tell you a lot about someone.

When you are talking with a prospective tenant, one of the most important things to find out is their source of income. Do they have a secure job? They should make good tenants if they have a good steady job. Ask about their hobbies. If they spend their spare time repairing cars in the front yard or motorcycle racing they may not be welcome by the neighbors. A band member who likes to jam with his friends at all hours of the night, might also cause problems with the neighbors. Ask if they like to throw parties. You can explain that you are looking for a quiet tenant.

The price you are asking for the rental is important. I was not getting much response on a small house I was renting when I advertised it for $1420. But when I lowered the price to $1395, the calls came in. Go figure. A few dollars in the rental market can make a difference.

Leveraging:

The beauty of all real estate is that you can "leverage" your investment. When you buy a property, typically you pay only a small percentage of the purchase price. You get a lender to finance the rest. This is called leveraging. You only have to put in a portion of the cost of the property.

Typically you put in 20% as a down payment when you buy real estate and you borrow the remainder. If the value of the property goes up, you get 100% of the appreciation even though you provided only 20% of the purchase price.

Here's how it works. If you buy a $200,000 rental property, you put in 20% down which is a payment of $40,000. You get a loan from a lender for $160,000 which has monthly mortgage payments of around $1,000. The rent from your tenant is about $1,200 which just about covers the mortgage plus property taxes and insurance.

The values of real estate do go up and down. But unlike more risky investments, if your property is in a growth area, it will always end up appreciating in value. In the US, the average real estate values went up 87% over the last 10 years, however they fell back down about 45% during the recent recession. Which means they still went up 42% over 10 years or an average of 4.2% per year – better than many other types of investments.

Highest return on your money:

Here's the good part. Looking at the previous example of the $200,000 rental property: Say you're located in a strong growth area and in the next year the property goes up 5% in value. That means it is now worth $210,000. So you have just earned $10,000 on your investment (down payment) of $40,000. That is a 25% return on your investment, which is equal to earning 25% annual interest.

Now where else can you earn such a high interest? In good times, in some places the real estate market has gone up 5% in as little as 6 months. That is a return of 50% per annum on your $40,000 investment. This is why so many millionaires are made in real estate.

Yes, you have to go through all the trouble of buying property, then finding a renter, etc. But for these kinds of returns, isn't it worth it? And you have a concrete investment. Something that can't be lost with the whim of stock manipulators. In my experience, if you hold on to property in a desirable location for the long term, it should go up in value and eventually be paid off by your tenants. What better investment is there?

Oh, you say, the real estate market has taken a dive in the last few years. Where I am in the San Diego real estate market, the values have gone down some 45 % recently. However they have gone up over 100% in the last 10 years. So the average now is a 55% increase – still a great investment if you bought years ago and held on.

Not such a good investment if you bought at the peak of the market. In that case, you'll have to hold on to it much longer to get an increase on your investment. But if you matched your purchase price to your rental income, as I advised you to do, then you're still okay. The tenant is buying the property for you.

So the goal in owning rental property is to have the rent payment cover the mortgage payment, that way you'll have the tenant buying the property for you.

Spread the risk:

"Don't put all your eggs into one basket." Where have you heard that before? You may not want to put all your own cash into one property. You may want to spread the risk. Then you should think about owning more than one rental property and use various investors who are each investing in just part of the various properties.

If one project is not working or is held up, then you have the others to fall back on. That way you can afford to wait until a particular property turns around. You don't need to panic sell if the market isn't doing well at this time. You want your investment in any particular property to be minimal.

Security in a partnership:

Some people are reluctant to take on partners because they feel that the partner is taking too much of the profits and without one they could keep all the profits for themselves. But this is wrong thinking. If the project is small and the profits are small, then sure you could do better on your own.

However, using partners allows you to acquire more valuable properties that offer much larger potential profits. Often you can make more money on a smaller share of a large project, than a 100% share on a small project. The idea is to use other peoples money to allow you to get into properties that you could never buy on your own.

Where to find investors:

There are many options for finding partners or investors. One is to advertise in your local newspaper or online classifieds. Find the sections called "Money Wanted" or "Financial Investments." Nowadays many investors are wary of the stock market and don't know where their money will earn a decent interest rate.

There should be people out there who would be interested in a first trust deed on a good residential rental property. You could offer an 8% interest rate to peak their interest. Some may want you to pay additional points for the loan, but if you are not working with a loan broker, you probably shouldn't have to.

To attract investors, you need to choose the right property and structure an appealing incentive package. You want to find out what interest rates investors expect to be paid and what properties are most desirable.

It is your job to make the proposal as attractive as possible to potential partners or investors. This means you need to show that the property is a real value in a very desirable area. You present comparable property values in the same neighborhood that are much higher than this wonderful bargain of yours.

In your presentation to the investor you may want to emphasize that right now is an ideal time to invest in real estate because it is still a buyers market and the prices are low. You want to impress on him or her that this is an opportune time to get a property that will allow a positive cash flow from the renter.

Tying up the property:

When you feel confident that you will be able to find a good investor, that's the time you want to take a leap and tie up the property you have been researching. You want to move ahead and present an offer to the seller and settle on the price and terms before you bring in your investor.

What you don't want to do, is make a full presentation to an investor on a property and get him or her all interested, only to find out that the seller won't take the deal or that the property is no longer available.

In most cases when you are making a pitch to an investor, you are talking about a specific property. You need to present its particulars, talking about the condition of the house, the quality of the neighborhood and especially its bargain value. If you haven't tied up the property in escrow, it may not even be there when the investor says yes.

It would be good to arrange an escrow period of at least sixty days to give you time to find the right investor. You will also need to put into the purchase contract a lot of contingencies to protect your deposit, if the investors don't pan out. You can write in as a contingency a partner's approval.

The technique of tying up a property in escrow is common for most real estate entrepreneurs. They tie up a bargain property, then go find the money. On a larger more expensive acreage project, the buyer will often tie it up for as long as six months while he does his "due diligence." That's a fancy term for looking up all the details about a property. The buyer will tell the seller that he needs time to research all the codes, soil and water studies, etc.– when actually he spends most of the time looking for money.

Real Estate Investment Trusts:

I thought I might mention here another alternative to investing in real estate. This may work for those of you who want to get into real estate but don't have much money to invest and don't want to get involved in the whole process of buying and/or managing properties.

A Real Estate Investment Trust (REIT) is a way for individuals to invest in real estate even if they have limited funds. A REIT is a group of small investors who pool their resources to buy real estate. The risk of loss is then spread out among all the investors.

To form a REIT there must be a minimum of 100 investors. But they are each putting in a limited amount of money. Typically the REIT will purchase many different properties to diversify their investment.

REIT's were originally created by the IRS to allow tax payers to qualify for certain tax provisions. A REIT is allowed to distribute to its members (investors) the greater part of its profits generated from the sale of its properties. The REIT itself does not pay taxes on its profits, but individual members of the trust are taxed at their own tax rates, on the dividends distributed to them. Generally REIT's distribute dividends to their members which can come from rental income from the many properties it owns.

This is not a bad place for the small investor to put his money as long as the principals are making wise investment decisions.

The demand will always be there:

The population of the United States is growing by over 3 million people a year. These people have to live someplace. It has been noted by the research firm Reis Inc. that new apartment construction in most parts of the country has fallen in past years. But the population keeps growing. The demand is there, particularly in growth areas. With fewer apartments and continuous growth, rents for landlords can only increase.

The areas of growing pockets of improvement in real estate investment these days may surprise you. As of the date of this writing, the data from the National Association of Home Builders has identified those metropolitan areas that have shown the most improvement in the key economic indexes – housing permits, employment and housing prices. They are as follows:

1. Alexandra, LA
2. Anchorage, AK
3. Bangor, ME
4. Bismarck, ND
5. Casper, WY
6. Fairbanks, AK
7. Fayetteville, NC
8. Houma, LA
9. Midland, TX
10. New Orleans, LA
11. Pittsburgh, PA
12. Waco, TX

Most of these cities, as you notice, are not the traditional sun-belt destinations. Those areas were descended on by developers who over-built creating large market swings and instability.

Remember land is a finite commodity and the population just keeps growing in good times or bad, so in the long run demand can only increase for real estate. And when demand increases, so do values.

CHAPTER SEVEN

WHERE THE MONEY IS

Unless you are doing a no money down purchase, in most real estate transactions you will need some cash as a down payment. Typically lenders, be they private or businesses, like to see at least 20% of the purchase price as a down payment. But what if you haven't got the cash? In this chapter I'll give you some ideas where to find this cash.

Credit Cards:

One obvious place for ready cash is credit cards. But because of their higher interest rates, it is important to be cautious. This option may be preferable if you just need a short term loan and plan to pay it off with another source of funds within a limited period of time.

An example of this may be if your uncle is willing to invest in your home purchase, but his money won't be available for four months. You really think you have found an ideal house and you want to buy it. The cash needed can be covered by a credit card, so you go ahead with the purchase. In four months your uncle's money comes through, so you are able to pay off the credit card.

There was a story about a real estate entrepreneur who obtained as many credit cards as he could to finance rental housing purchases. For a while he thought he was sitting on top of the world with many good rental properties. But as these stories go, all the monthly payments on all those credit cards got the best of him and he had to declare bankruptcy. This is a cautionary tale for all of us.

Money from a business:

One idea for raising cash is to use your business, if you have one, for the many types of money programs available. If you haven't got a business, you could try creating a side business of your own to supplement your income and give you some start-up working capital as well.

Here is a story of such an idea: Jake had a relatively good job that earned him an adequate income. But as most of us experience, he had nothing left at the end of the month for any savings. He felt like he was going to be stuck as a renter for the rest of his life.

Then a friend of Jake told him how he could earn extra income, part time, on the internet. Jake took up the challenge and worked on various approaches. After some trial and error, he finally settled into selling items on ebay and other web sites. He was able to buy these items wholesale overseas using the internet. And after a while he was able to turn a profit. With his side business, Jake was finally able to start putting money aside for a house purchase.

Another person, call her Jane, was in the same situation. She had a job that only paid her bills. She was unable to save enough for her dream of owning her own home. Her biggest expense was the rent she paid on her apartment. She thought about it for awhile and came up with the idea that if she could cut her rent in half then the remaining money would give her what she needed for her savings.

She decided to take in a roommate to share the cost of the apartment. This also allowed her to cut her utility bills in half. This included; internet, cable TV, electricity and water. She put the saved money away in a savings account each month and soon she was on her way to buying her first modest house.

Home office:

Once you have gained the capital you need to purchase and move into a home, you may think about using the home as a business location. If you have a new start-up business, it could be conducted out of your new home.

There are some good savings that should be made from this.

When you are using your home for business, set aside a specific room as your home office where you will run the business. The IRS may allow you to use this room as a tax deduction. The way this is done is you calculate what percentage of your house square footage this room entails. Say it is 20% of your house. Then you may be able to deduct 20% of the house expenses from your taxable income. These expenses could include utilities, maintenance, a portion of your mortgage, etc.

A place for a tenant:

Here is an idea that has served me well. This can help earn you extra money to pay the mortgage. When you buy your new home, figure out where you could carve out a space that will allow you to rent out a small part of your house to a tenant. This space could be an extra bedroom and bathroom that you don't need. You will want to create an exterior entrance to this space and a place for a small kitchenette.

To put together a kitchenette, you'll need to buy a range, refrigerator and a sink cabinet with faucet. You'll need to hire a plumber to hook up the sink. You can buy the appliances used on Craigslist. The money spent should be returned to you with a few months of rental income.

The goal here is to have a room that provides the tenant with their own place separate from the rest of the house. You are not sharing your house. The tenant should be in their own space with their own kitchen and bath. You want them to be able to come and go without disturbing you. You should close off any interior door that may connect the tenant's space with the rest of the house.

This type of rental is ideal for a single young girl or boy who are starting out in the world. Often they are a college student and don't want to live in a noisy apartment house. Be sure to screen them well. You want a quiet computer worm not a party animal. Sometimes there is an older person with very limited income that will fit the bill, as long as they don't need your constant help with everything they do.

Free Money:

Much of what I will be discussing here might seem to be off the subject of house financing, but I thought it might be helpful information to know because it relates to looking for start up capital for a business.

In looking for start-up capital, one option can be found in grants or low interest loans available from both the Federal Government and private money sources. Setting up low income rental housing may be an option for a new start-up business that might qualify for a grant.

Grants are free money not loans. They never have to be paid back. Their purpose is to help the small-business owner get a leg up to start a new business. Small businesses are the backbone of our economy. They are the largest employers – employing over 60% of the U.S.

workforce. The government wants to encourage new businesses as much as possible.

Programs for grants are always fluid. They change often. So it is important for you to do your research and adjust your business to fit current requirements.

The internet is the information source for everything you will need to know. And to find grants, you should not have to pay for access to online databases. You can find all these online sources for free, if you know where to look. And this is what I will help you with.

Government web sites:

Perhaps the best site for finding grants from the Federal Government is www.govbenefits.gov . This site is easy to navigate and presents thousands of grant programs. If you are not sure what programs you might qualify for, go to the "Start Here" button and fill in the questionnaire. These are simple, easy to answer questions. Once answered, the programs will pop-up that you might be eligible for.

Another resource is www.grants.gov. Every government agency that has grants is listed here. There are as many as one thousand grant programs presented with many billions of dollars in available funds. You can start by browsing through all the different programs. No need to register until you're ready to apply for a grant.

Another government site is www.grantsolutions.gov. This site states that it distributes over $200 billion in grants each year. Parts of the research and development budgets for NASA and other departments are allocated to grants to small businesses that can provide them with projects they deem useful.

SBA loans:

If you would like to pursue a low interest loan for your business, then try www.govloans.gov. The Small Business Administration (SBA) has programs that provide start-up businesses with loan guarantees at low interest rates and high "loan to value" (LTV).

As I discussed earlier, LTV is used in real estate loans. You may recall that it refers to the amount of loan that the lender will give in relation to the appraised value of real estate. SBA also gives *unsecured* start-up loans. These are loans that are not secured by real estate.

The SBA also coordinates for other government agencies that award grants for such things as high-tech. ventures. The SBA can be found at www. sba.gov. There are many businesses out there that got their start with government loans or venture capital.

Another government agency, Small Business Investment Company (SBIC) provides venture capital to small businesses that are intent on growing. And this agency will help almost any type of business. They can be reached at: www.sba.gov/aboutsba/sbaprograms/inv/index.html. SBIC has billions of government funds to allocate as well as private funding.

Private Money:

There are private foundations that also give grants and low cost loans for all kinds of projects. Here are some web sites you can check out:
- www.foundationcenter.org / fundfinders /
- www.fundsnetservice.com

For a directory of most of the private charitable foundations that give grants, go to www.foundations.org / grantmakers.html. Here you'll find a comprehensive list of people and organizations who have grants for almost everything. You may also type "private foundation grants" into your search engine. But beware, there are a lot of profiteers out there asking for your money to give you the same information you can get for free at these web sites.

Writing grants:

Don't be intimidated about writing for a grant. Remember that many grant seekers are no different from you. And besides, what harm can it do? The worst thing they can say is "sorry we chose someone else." You just refine your proposal and go after another grant.

You may need to organize your business so that it fits the criteria of the grant you are seeking. Some grants may require some experience you don't have. Then you find partners with that experience who will beef up your proposal.

When writing for a grant, write with enthusiasm. You want the people who are offering the grant to feel your optimism and energy. This should draw their attention to you and make them interested in your application. The technique in writing here is to first put down on scratch paper anything you can think of regarding the business you are creating. Then you can edit it several times and fine tune it later.

Grant applications need to show that you are organized and clear thinking, so a lot of editing is good. Get help from friends. The grant foundations and agencies expect to see your proposal well written and carefully thought out. Again don't be intimidated. You may be the only applicant that fits in with what they are looking for. It would be a shame not to have at least tried.

Business credit:

A good source of funding that many new business owners may not be aware of is credit that is readily offered to business. Even if your personal credit lines are in bad shape with a poor credit history, you may still qualify for business credit cards under the name of the business, particularly if it is a corporation. Have the business name unrelated to your name and acquire a Federal tax business I.D. number.

One of the best ways to start over if you have bad credit, is to incorporate. As a corporation you get a fresh credit history, tax advantages and protection of your personal assets. And accessing new credit lines is perhaps the best reason to incorporate.

With a new business you can immediately start off with good credit. Your business gets a new corporate tax I.D. number and does not use your personal social security number. You are establishing a new credit history with this new tax I.D. number and your business credit score will be unrelated to your personal credit score.

Getting credit for a brand new company could be tricky, but there are credit card companies that will extend credit. Seeing that you are a promising new business is all they seem to need. There are also credit-builder companies available on the internet who promise to help new businesses find credit right away. They will likely charge a fee, so be sure that you are working with a reputable company.

Another bonus is that interest rates on business credit cards are lower than interest rates on personal credit cards. And the interest on a business card may be tax deductible, which is not true of your personal credit cards.

Loans from individuals:

Though I mention using relatives as partners in a real estate purchase, as an alternative, you could just ask them for a loan. You could borrow cash from relatives or people you know. If you present your new business plans well drawn up and well organized, then you might be surprised at how well your ideas are received.

There are a lot of options in the world of finance. Don't be discouraged if one idea doesn't pan out, as you can see here there are many other options for you to work with.

Our friend, the IRS?

Saving on taxes is one way to keep your money. When doing your income taxes you may have noticed that there are such things as *tax credits*. These are not the same as tax deductions. Tax credits are given for such things as buying a Hybrid car or making your home more energy efficient. Such things as replacing old windows, updating the furnace or installing new insulation – all may be eligible for tax credits. These not just save on your taxes but also your energy bill.

The IRS actually has a long list of possible tax credits. Chances are you should be eligible for some of them. You can go online to their website at www.irs.gov to find what is available. For example, a solar hot water system may get you a tax credit of up to two thousand dollars. Another website for this information is www.energystar. gov . Here they have all the latest information on energy saving tax credits.

For your family, presently there are tax credits of one thousand dollars for each of your children. There is also the earned income tax credit which is designed for low income workers. IRS Publication 96 will explain how this works. Tax credits are like receiving free money. Any money you can keep is as good as money you can earn.

Keeping your money:

Getting free or cheap money is good, but keeping it is just as good. You must learn how to hold onto your money. In this consumer driven society, it is very easy for money to disappear month after month, especially if you overextend yourself. Sometimes it can feel as if the more money you make, the more you spend. So the balance is still zero at the end of the month.

How To Save:

Since the biggest stumbling block to buying a home is usually money, it is important to learn how to deal with money, particularly how to save it. Over the years I have seen too many promising entrepreneurs over spend and over extend themselves into a pile of debts they could not repay. This is not a path you want to take.

It is generally not an easy task to save your money. It can seem like paying all the bills consumes all of your paycheck. Financial experts are always telling us to make a budget for our expenditures. But most people just can't do it. Budgets usually don't work because they are difficult to live with.

It is uncomfortable working your way through budgets, crunching the numbers every month. And it is rather depressing when you find you can't stick to it. It seems to go against our very nature to have to deprive ourselves financially, even if it is for a good cause like saving to buy a home.

Pay Yourself First:

There is a technique that is better than budgeting. It is called "Paying Yourself First." What this means is that when you receive your paycheck – before you pay any other bills – you put money aside for yourself.

The natural way people respond when they get paid is to first pay the bills. Then if something is left over, they put it into a savings account. They pay everyone else first and themselves last. This is a mistake. What happens is that there usually is nothing left over. Somehow even if there is some cash floating around, it tends to disappear with all those small expenditures.

Putting money aside for yourself is not being on a budget. Because no matter what the situation is that month, this money is saved, rain or shine. You pay yourself first before you pay a dime to anything else.

I am not suggesting a lot of money here, the technique works with setting aside as little as 10 % (or even less) of your income. This may come to just a few dollars per day. If you pay attention to your expenditures, you'll find these same dollars are now being spent on things that you can easily do without – those expensive lattes for example.

Why is this technique any good, you ask? Because this small bit of income, if set aside month after month, year after year can actually grow to enough money to help purchase your first home. Of course this is dependant on you starting at a young enough age.

A steady approach:

Not a lot of people these days are able to raise enough money to buy a home. The beauty of a technique like "paying yourself first" is that with a few simple steps each month, you can build up your savings. This is the slow and steady approach to your goal, but with every month your savings account grows and grows.

CHAPTER EIGHT

YOUR PATH TO SUCCESS

To be successful in buying real estate, you need a number of elements to fall into place. But all these elements are dependant on you. As I mentioned in previous chapters, you need to do your homework. You need to research all the possible locations that appeal to you and give you the best value for your investment. You should look at all the possible houses that will work within your budget and figure out the best way to finance the one you like. You, or those helping you, will need to negotiate with the seller to get the best possible deal. And you will need to stay positive and optimistic through it all.

This last part is sometimes the hardest to achieve – to remain upbeat and sure of success even after being turned down by a number of prospects. It can be hard to keep going if you can't find what you are looking for. Some people will go out and look at a number of houses and not find any financing and they give up and resign themselves to a life as a renter. But this is not the way you want to be.

Persistence:

There are a lot of houses out there for sale. You will find what you are looking for, only you have to keep at it. All great success stories involve someone who kept at it, someone who was persistent, even after many failures. Edison, who invented the light bulb, tried something like two thousand filaments before he found one that finally worked. J. K. Rowling who wrote the Harry Potter series, was turned down by publisher after publisher, but kept going anyway, until she finally found one. Persistence was an important part of their success.

The desire to succeed:

One thing that is found in people who are persistent, is a strong desire to succeed. This desire can be consciously developed through techniques such as focusing on a goal. There are many self-help books out there that talk about visualizing your goal. Olympic athletes are trained to visualize themselves being successful in whatever competition they are involved in. And it works or they wouldn't be still doing it competition after competition.

Many of the most powerful and successful people in the world will tell you that they put a lot of focus and attention on those things they want to attain and achieve.

Successful thinking:

Your thinking has a lot to do with how successful you are. There have been a good number of studies that have shown that people's thinking habits directly relate to their achievements or lack thereof. They found that people with positive thinking are better able to achieve their goals. People with negative thinking are often disappointed with their achievements. Which of course adds to their negative attitude.

If a person is constantly repeating thoughts like: "I can never get ahead" or "I never have enough money," there are probably going to be some problems in their life. What you are thinking most of the time will automatically affect your actions or inactions. If you are telling yourself that: "Life can only get better" or "I have all the support I need to succeed," your actions will naturally reflect this attitude and you will be pushing successfully toward your goal.

What you are constantly telling yourself is feeding into the subconscious. And the more you hear the same type of thinking, the more your subconscious believes it as true. Repetition creates a sense of validity. Advertisers and politicians know this. The more you hear something, the more real it becomes. So do you want to believe "I can never succeed" or "I can always succeed?" It is your choice.

Ingrained habits:

A lot of our thinking habits are what we were raised with. As children we naturally mimicked the behavior of our parents or older siblings. To some extent we tended to repeat what they said or acted the way they acted. And at school our thinking was shaped by teachers and other students with either good or harmful results. Some of the results of our childhood created some harmful limitations on our ability to succeed.

Here is a story to show what I mean: Some years ago, my wife and I were visiting the Wild Animal Park in San Diego. The place is beautiful. They have made a great effort to create spacious and comfortable habitats for all the animals there.

We were walking by one large space that was well landscaped. However the tiger there kept pacing back and forth on the same path using only about twenty feet of his spacious habitat. We concluded that this magnificent animal was probably raised elsewhere in a cage no larger than the space he was pacing back and forth in. He was oblivious to all the beautiful new space he had been given.

In some ways all of us have been raised within limits starting from infancy. We continue to act in a confined manner with limited thinking. We have trouble setting goals that are higher than those we were raised with. We may find it difficult to set out on a path that no one we know has tried.

You talk too much:

I used to know a guy who had to tell everyone, everything he was thinking of. He would have an idea for a new career and he would discuss it with anyone and everyone he ran into. Even some stranger in a café. Yet he never quiet got around to doing anything. You probably know the type. They call them "all talk and no action."

Well what we decided was that all the energy that he had, that would have gone into creating his new career, was completely dissipated with all that talk. It takes a certain amount creative energy to start up a business or work out alternative financing to buy a new home. You may find that if you discuss it too much, with too many people, then the energy just sort of disappears or even worse, you now feel drained. This leads to another subject about how those around us influence our actions.

A little help from my friends:

Our friends can have a significant influence on how we think and how we act. We can all use a supportive friend that encourages us to make the most of ourselves – someone who is there helping to promote our ideas, motivating and inspiring us to go forward.

But that doesn't necessarily include all our friends. Recently I saw a study that showed that over 80% of women and over 70% of men admit that they have a "toxic" friend. A majority of these people said that these were likely to be their *best* friends and that they were likely to continue their relationship with them.

Your friend is someone you really like and hang out with. Someone you share confidences with. But a toxic friend may also be feeding your thinking with subtle and not so subtle doubts about yourself and your abilities.

They may insert some comments such as: "Are you sure you want to invest in a house at this time, my cousin lost a lot of money on his house." or "Nobody with any sense is buying property now, better to wait." Yes, wait until the prices go back up and it becomes a sellers market and all the good deals are gone.

Toxic friends are not helpful in achieving your dreams. It seems that if they can't do it, then why should you. They will tell stories about someone who couldn't make a go of it. But the last thing you need now is a steady diet of failure stories to undermine your hopes and dreams.

A supportive friend will always encourage you and help you have strong positive thinking about your goal of owning your own home. When you are all excited about some place that you have found, you need to hear some cheerful encouragement from those around you. This adds to your resolve to make the house become a reality.

Where do we go from here?

So if we do find ourselves with thinking that is not helping with our success, what do we do? We should try to figure out where these bad thought habits come from. If you are being fed negative statements from so-called friends, then it might be better to avoid discussing your hopes and dreams with them. If you think the thoughts are ingrained in your head from a lifetime of listening to family, school, etc., then you'll need to take an alternative approach.

Psychologists have found that we all tend to carry on a silent dialogue with ourselves throughout the day. What I found to be effective is to try to stop and listen to what you are telling yourself. If you don't like what you hear, then right there and then change the thought to an opposite positive statement. If you find yourself saying "I never seem to have enough money," then change it to "I have all the money I need."

It doesn't matter if the reality out there doesn't seem to support this idea. It may take a lot of repetition of your new statement to counter all the previous negative repetitions. But after a while, your subconscious will begin to believe your new statement and you'll find that things will turn around. You'll be more motivated to act towards achieving your goal, be it having more money or finding that ideal home with the financing you need.

Picture Perfect:

Another technique for achieving success may seem rather odd, but it has been proven to work. Here is an example: Many years ago I happened to pick up a brochure at a car dealership. I really liked the look of a teal blue sports car that was on the cover of the brochure, so I hung it on the wall of my office.

Some time passed. I was selling a house that I had built and a call came from a real estate agent. She asked if I would be interested in a sports car as a down payment on the house. When she described the car, I almost fell out of my seat. It was the exact car I had hung on the wall. It was the same color, same model, same year, everything. Naturally I said yes.

I later found out that others had successfully used this technique to get what they wanted. Did you know that Kate Middletown hung a poster of Prince William on her wall when she was growing up? Princess Diana had done the same thing with Charles' picture. Actually there are books written about this visualization technique.

So now I have an assignment for you. Draw a rough image of what you think your ideal house would look like. Be practical, don't draw a palace. And it isn't necessary to be too specific. Now write under this picture "my house." Hang it where you can see it. And know that you will have your house, one way or another.

If there is a house out there that you always wanted, take a photo of it and put it up on the wall. You never know what could happen. Sometimes it takes time, but if you combine the picture with a positive statement that you are repeating to yourself, I think you will be pleased with the results.

A successful start:

This book is the beginning of your road to success in buying your new home. You have been shown many different ways you can find, finance and purchase that home you've been hoping for.

I wrote this book because I was able to successfully use a number of these techniques to buy properties. I want you to have the same success. You can go ahead now and try out some of these techniques. They do work. There are sellers out there that are anxious to hear from you and they may be very willing to work with your ideas. You could be doing them a great favor.

Just by reading this book, you've shown that you are already working to make progress toward your goal. From here you just take one step after another. Step by step, your goal is closer. Sometimes it may take a number of tries, but if you keep at it, with persistence, you will be successful.